A Love Story from the Desert:
Majnūn Leyla

Arabic Text, Commentary and Translations

Arabic
Love Poetry
from the Desert:
Majnūn Leyla

Arabic Text, Commentary and Translations

Joyce Åkesson

Pallas Athena

Lund

2012

ALSO BY JOYCE ÅKESSON

Arabic Proverbs and Wise Sayings, Pallas Athena Distribution, October 2011.

Causes and Principles in Arabic, Pallas Athena Distribution, June 2011.

A Study of Arabic Phonology, Pallas Athena Distribution, August 2010.

The Basics & Intricacies of Arabic Morphology, Pallas Athena Distribution, July 2010.

The Phonological Changes due to the Hamza and Weak Consonant in Arabic, Pallas Athena Distribution, April 2010.

A Study of the Assimilation and Substitution in Arabic, Pallas Athena Distribution, March 2010.

The Essentials of the Class of the Strong Verb in Arabic, Pallas Athena Distribution, January 2010

The Complexity of the Irregular Verbal and Nominal Forms & the Phonological Changes in Arabic, Pallas Athena Distribution, April 2009.

Arabic Morphology and Phonology: Based on the Marāḥ al-Arwāḥ by Aḥmad b. ᶜAlī b. Masᶜūd, Studies in Semitic Languages and Linguistics, Brill Academic Publishers, July 2001.

Aḥmad B. ᶜAlī B. Masᶜūd on Arabic Morphology, Marāḥ al-Arwāḥ: Part 1: The Strong Verb, Studia Orientalia Lundensia, Vol. 4, Brill Academic Publishers, October 1990.

POETRY

Majnūn Leyla: Poems about Passion, Pallas Athena Distribution, December 2009.

The Invitation, Pallas Athena Distribution, July 2009.

Love's Thrilling Dimensions, Pallas Athena Distribution, February 2009.

Table of Contents

Introduction XI

The Poems 1

O you morning bird 9

ألا لا أحب السير إلا مصعدا (5)

I only want to travel if the road takes me northward 11

منعت عن التسليم يوم وداعها (6)

They forbade me to visit her on the day that she traveled 13

إذا نظرت نحوي تكلم طرفها (7)

If she looked my way her eyes talked to me 15

أشارت بعينيها مخافة أهلها (8)

She gave me a sign with her eyes of fear of her parents 17

وما الناس إلا العاشقون ذو الهوى (9)

The good persons are only those who can love 19

زها جسم ليلى في الثياب تنعما (10)

Your whole body in its garment is radiant in its beauty and gaiety, O Leyla 21

ليالي أصبو بالعشي وبالضحى (11)

When the night falls and the dawn breaks, I dream 23

هي الخمر في حسن وكالخمر ريقها (12)

Her beauty is like wine, her saliva and its clarity too 25

ومما شجاني أنها يوم ودعت (13)

O the worst of misery! Our farewell day 27

أحبك يا ليلى وأفرط في حبي (14)

I love you, O my Leyla, I persist on loving you 29

وأجهشت للتوباد حين رأيته (15)

When I saw the mountain of Tawbād, my heart was seized by sorrow 31

أمن أجل خيمات على مدرج الصبا (16)

Is it the camp's fault that it is situated in the Orient 33

أمر على الديار ديار ليلى (17)

When I pass by the house, Leyla's house 35

أبوس تراب رجلك يا لويلى (18)

I kiss the earth on which your foot has stepped, O soft Leyla 37

أتضرب ليلى كلما زرت دارها (19)

Must they hit Leyla every time that I visit her dwelling? 39

يقولون لي يوما وقد جئت حيهم (20)

They asked me once when I came to visit their quarter 41

أيا ليلى بكى لي بعينيك رحمة (21)

Both of us know, O Leyla, that you have cried of compassion
and love over me 43

أهابك إجلالا (22)

I honor you and fear you 45

ألا هل طلوع الشمس يهدي تحية (23)

You shall greet, O sun 47

مليحة أطلال العشيات لو بدت (24)

O the remains of the camp, O the soft presence 49

يقولون ليلى بالعراق مريضة (25)

They say: "Leyla is in Iraq and is sick 51

أقول لأصحابي هي الشمس (26)

I say to my friends: "She is the sun 55

رعاة الليل (27)

O night's shepherds 57

لا يا نسيم الريح حكمك جائر (28)

You treat me so badly, O soft breeze 61

فيا قلب مت حزنا ولا تك جازعا (29)

Do not suffer, O loving heart, but rather die quickly filled with sorrow 63

فوالله ثم والله إني لدائب (30)

Help me, O my God, I think of her all the time! 67

أموت إذا شطت وأحيا إذا دنت (31)

I die if she goes away, I live if she comes near 71

أما والذي أرسى ثبيرا مكانه (32)

I swear by Him Who chose to live over the Thabīr mountain 73

وجدت الحب نيرانا (33)

Love, I see it well, is a glowing fire 75

بنفسي من لا بد لي أن أهاجره (34)

She whom I ought to forget lives in my soul 77

يميل بي الهوى في أرض ليلى (35)

To Leyla's country passion takes me 81

ألا أيها القصاد نحوي (36)

O you who are persecuting me 83

وإنك لو بلغتها قولي اسلمى (37)

If you send her my greeting 85

أظن هواها تاركي بمضلة (38)

My love for her, I believe, forces me to wander 87

ألا أيها القلب الذي لج هائما (39)

Poor crazy heart in its love 89

ألا يا غراب البين (40)

O you crow, bird of absence 91

أقول لمفت ذات يوم لقيته (41)

I asked a mufti whom I met on that day 93

وداع دعا إذ نحن بالخيف من منى (42)

We were in Minā, in al-Khayf. A man shouted out a name 95

حججت ولم أحجج لذنب جنيته (43)

I did not beg during this pilgrimage to make amends for a sin
that I have committed 97

ذكرتك والحجيج لهم ضجيج (44)

The pilgrims gather around me... In this noise, among all these
people, my glowing thoughts go to you 99

ذكرتك حيث استأمن الوحش (45)

In this place in which the beasts are safe 101

أيا جبلي نعمان بالله خليا (46)

O Naᶜmān's two mountains, by God you must allow 103

متى يشتفي منك الفؤاد المعذب (47)

When shall my tormented heart ever be healed from you? 105

إليك عني هائم وصب (48)

Abandon me to my crazy wandering! 107

حلال لليلى شتمنا وانتقاصنا (49)

What slanders are poisoning Leyla's soul? 109

وأنت التي كلفتني دلج السرى (50)

O you who have forced me to take a journey in the night 111

ما بال قلبك يا مجنون قد خلعا (51)

Contemplate, O poor madman, this heart snatched away 113

أحن إلى أرض الحجاز (52)

I long for the earth of Al-Ḥidjāz 115

سلبت عظامي لحمها فتركتها (53)

My bones have not longer any skin, you have undressed them 117

نظرت كأني من وراء زجاجة (54)

I looked at the camp and I thought that I was seeing it behind a glass pane 119

وقفت لليلى بعد عشرين حجة (55)

I shall not go farther away, O Leyla, twenty years, this is a too long time 121

عجبت لليلى كيف نامت وقد غفت (56)

I am surprised that Leyla can fall asleep 123

أَلا تلك ليلى قد أَلم لمامها (57)

Leyla is now mine 125

تذكرت ليلى والسنين الخواليا (58)

I remember, O Leyla, the years that passed and all these

days! 127

أَرقت وعادني هم جديد (59)

Sleep left me and opened the way for new torments 145

أيا قبر ليلى (60)

O Leyla's grave 147

لو سيل أهل الهوى من بعد موتهم (61)

If beyond death one asked the lovers 149

أَلا ليتنا كنا غزالين نرتعي (62)

I wish we were two deer grazing 151

Introduction

This collection of Arabic love poems is attributed to Qays b. al-Mulawwaḥ, also known as Majnūn al-ᶜĀmirī "The Madman from the tribe of Banū ᶜĀmir" and Majnūn Leyla "the one who was obsessed or mad about Leyla". He was from the Banū ᶜĀmir tribe in the northern Arabian Peninsula and lived during the Ummayad era in the 7th century. He fell in love with his cousin Leylā bint Mahdīy (d. 688), better known as Leyla al-ᶜĀmirīya. They were both from the same tribe and used to spend a lot of time together, tending their parents' flocks in a mountain called al-Tawbād. Leyla returned Qays' love quietly while Qays became so obsessively in love with her that he started to write romantic passionate poems about her. When Qays' poetry became very famous and the people started to discuss them and recite them, Leyla's parents became very annoyed about all the noise that they caused around her and decided to marry her to Ward b. Muḥammad in order to save her reputation. Qays became then desperate and known as Majnūn Leyla "driven mad by Leyla". He spent his time in the desert and refused to marry any woman. Leyla moved with her husband to Iraq where she became ill and eventually died. Upon hearing the news of her death, Qays emerged from the wilderness to visit her grave. He was later found dead in 688 near it. He had carved three verses of poetry on a rock near the grave, and they were the last three verses attributed to him.

The early stories and poems about Majnūn Layla were documented in different Arabic collections, the most well-known being *Basṭ ṣamiᶜ al-Masāmir* by Muḥammad b. ᶜAlī b. Maḥmūd b. Ṭūlūn (d. 953), the encyclopedic collection of over 20 volumes, the *Kitāb al-Aghānī "The Book of Songs"* by the Arab litterateur of Qurayshī origin, Abu'l-Faraj al-Aṣfahānī (d. 967) and the *Maṣāriᶜ al-ᶜushshāq* by Jaᶜfar b. Aḥmad al-Sarrāj (d. 1106). A more recent Arabic edition exists too, namely *Dīwān Majnūn Leyla* by ᶜAbd al-Sattār Farrāj.

Qays' and Leyla's love story spread and has been told in legends, songs, poems, plays and epics extending from the Caucasus to Africa and from the Atlantic to the Indian Ocean. It is a story of endless love, much like the later stories of Tristan and Isolde and Romeo and Juliet in Europe.

Majnūn Leyla's Arabic poems are known to belong to the genre of the *ash ᶜār al-ghazal al-ᶜudhrī* "platonic or virginal love poems", which emphasize on the spiritual love as opposed to *ash ᶜār al-ghazal* "erotic poems", which emphasize on the woman's physical beauty and on the desire that it arouses in her lover.

The main body of the present book is a presentation of 62 Arabic poems in the original from the 7th century. Each poem has a translation on the facing page. The English text has footnotes referring to comments that are placed at the end of the work.

The work provides insights into themes that were prevalent in the *ash ᶜār al-ghazal al-ᶜudhrī* "platonic or virginal love poems" during the Ummayad era and onwards. The main ones are an incurable romanticism, the deepest longings of the heart for its beloved, nostalgia, memories of a lost paradise, idealism, anticipation, joy after a reunion, bitterness after a separation, lovesickness, wandering in the desert and a consuming passion. The beloved, Leyla, is elevated and appears superior to everyone else. Although Majnūn is a faithful Muslim who performs pilgrimage, it is Leyla that he is most faithful to.

The Classical Arabic poems are known for using a complicated play with words that can have double meanings or different ambiguous meanings. The verses are rhymed and measured and follow one of the sixteen different established meters. The meters are known as *buḥūr* "seas", and each unit of the seas is known as *tafᶜīla*. As there is a certain number of *tafᶜīlas* in every sea, the measuring procedure of a poem is very rigorous, and sometimes only the fact of adding or removing a consonant or a vowel can shift the verse from one meter to another. Also every verse has to end with the same rhyme throughout the poem. These complexities may in themselves explain how impossible it is to get the same rhythm in the English translation. A literal translation of the poems is hence impossible as there are words and expressions that are acceptable in a language and heavy and unacceptable in another.

I have indicated the poem's meter and the last rhyme in the notes. In the case of a changeable consonant, I have used the sign &. In order to explain the contents of a specific poem I have in some cases introduced its background. I have referred in the notes to the different works from which each poem is selected and I have commented on a few issues whenever I felt that this was necessary. It is my hope that this book can offer to the reader a feeling of the poems' contents and structures.

I would like to extend my heartfelt appreciation to my friends and family, in particular, to my mother, Irene Egeland, my brother, James Hakim, my husband, Anders, and my son, Filip.

THE POEMS

(1)

وقالـوا لـو تشاءُ سلَـوْتَ عنهـا   فقـــلتَ لهـــمْ فإنِّـــى لا أشَاءُ

وكيــف وحبُّهـا عَلِــقٌ بقلْبــى   كمــا عَلِــقَتْ بأُرْشِيَـةٍ دِلاءُ

لهـا حبٌّ تَــنَشَّأَ فـى فــؤادى   فليس له ــ وإنْ زُجِرَ ــ انتِهاءُ

وعاذِلـــةٍ تُقَطِّعُنِـــى مَلامًـــا   وفـى زَجْـر العـواذِل لـى بـلاءُ

_____

They told me: "If you want

you can forget her!"

But I said: "I do not want and I cannot

because my love for her is tied to my heart

like the well bucket to the cord!

Of this endless love my soul knows the power!

But they mock me,

they scold me

and they drive me away

because they know

that their slanders destroy me![1]

(2)

وأرواحُها إن كان نجدٌ على العهدِ	ألا حبَّـذا نجـــدٌ وطـــيبُ ترابهـــا
لِطولِ التَّنائى هـل تَغَيَّرتَـا بعـدى	ألا ليتَ شِعرى عـن عُوَارِضَتَنْى قَـا
إذا هـو أُمسَى لَيْلَةً بثَرَى جَعْدِ	وعـن أُقْحُـوانِ الرمـلِ مـا هـو فاعـلُ
على عهدِنا أم لم تدوما على عَهْدِ	وعـن جارتِنـا بالبَتِيـل إلـى الْحِمَـى
بريح الْخُزَامَى هل تهبّ إلى نجد	وعـن عُلْوِيَّـاتِ الريـاح إذا جـرتْ
على لاحقِ المتنين مُنْدلِق الوَخْدِ	وهل أنفضَنَّ الدهرَ أفنـانَ لِثْتـى
ئطالَعُ من وَهْدٍ خصيب إلى وَهْدِ	وهل أسْمعنَّ الدهرَ أصواتَ هَجْمـة

Majnūn met a man who was coming from Najd. He started questioning him about Leyla and Najd. After that, he recited these verses while he was crying.

O Najd's wonders!

Oh, how fragrant is Najd's earth

and its people if Najd is still the same!

When can I praise Qanā's two mountains?

I have been for too long separated from them,

I do not dare more to believe that everything is still the same!

I think of you too when the evening falls,

you, daisy of the sands, damp from the soft dew of dawn,

how did you endure the night?

And you, young women, have you moved somewhere else

or are you still living there between al-Batīl[2] and al-Ḥimā?

I think of the wind that smells lavender and that is blowing there.

Will it pass by Najd?

Oh may I feel it again playing in my free and wild hair,

when I am riding a horse with thin sides that is speeding!

May I be able to hear in the green meadows

from valley to valley, our camels groan![3]

(3)

بحبك يا ليلى قد أصبحتُ شُهْرَةً   وكـلُّ بمـا ألقـاه عنـدكِ يَفهــمُ

صريعٌ من الـحب المبرِّح والجوى   وأيُّ فتًى من لوعـة البيـن يَسْلَـمُ

ومـا هـى إلاَّ حسرةٌ بعـد نظـرة   أثارتْ لهيبا فى الـحشاشة يُضْرَمُ

فـلا تقتلينـى بـالصدود وبالقِلـى   ومثـلكِ يـا ليلى يـرقُّ ويَرحـم

فـوالله إنَّـى فـيك عـانٍ وعـاشقٌ   أذوب غراما فيك والـحبَّ أكتـم

مخافـة واشٍ أو رقـيبٍ وحـاسد   يُحدِّث ما لا كانت الناس تعلم

―――――――――――

My love for you, O Leyla,

has made me famous,

and the whole world has heard

about the misery I am going through.

Suffocated by a cruel passion,

abandoned to despair, I suffer.

Who can rescue me?

Leyla, O my longing!

Oh you whose gaze

has ignited this tormenting fire in my heart!

Do not hate me

because I'll die if you drive me away!

Are you Leyla?

Then be considerate and tender.

I am your prisoner,

I love you,

by God, believe me!

My soul is revived by this love that I conceal

from fear of a slanderer or an envious spy,

who would reveal to the people

everything they did not know.[4]

(4)

تَحَمَّـلْ سَلاَمِـى لا تَذَرْنِـى مُنَادِيَـا   أَلاَ أَيُّهـا الطَّيْـرُ المُحَلِّـقُ غَادِيَـا

إلى بَلَدٍ إنْ كُنْتَ بـالْأَرْضِ هَادِيَـا   تَحَمَّـلْ هَـدَاك اللهُ مِنِّـى رِسَالـةً

بهـا الْقَـلْبُ مِنِّـى مُوثَـقٌ وفُؤَادِيَـا   إلى قَفْرَةٍ مِنْ نَحْوِ لَيْلَـى مَضَلَّـةٍ

تَـزَوَّدْتُ ذاك الْيـوْمَ آخِـرَ زَادِيَـا   أَلاَ لَيْتَ يَوْمًا حَلَّ بِى مِنْ فِرَاقِكُـمْ

O you morning bird,

fly away and carry my greeting to her.

Let me hope when I call out.

May God lead you forward to her!

If you return to the earth,

let it be to Leyla's country,

- a desert in which one gets lost,

but which ties my soul

and heart in its knot -.

Oh! I dream of a day

when nothing separates us.

I live of that dream,

it is my final hope![5]

(5)

أَلاَ لاَ أُحِبُّ السَّيْـــرَ إِلاَّ مُصَعِّـــدَا   وَلاَ البَـرْقَ إِلاَّ أَنْ يَكُـــونَ يَمَانِيَـــا

عَلَى مِثْـل لَيْلَى يَقْتُلُ المَرْءُ نَـفْسَهُ   وَإِنْ كُنْتُ مِنْ لَيْلَى عَلَى الْيَأْسِ طَاوِيَا

إِذَا مَا تَمَنَّى النَّاسُ رَوْحًا وَرَاحَـــةً   تَمَنَّيْتُ أَنْ أَلْقَاكِ يَا لَيْلَ خَالِيَـا

أَرَى سَقَمًا فِي الْجِسْمِ أَصْبَحَ ثَاوِيَا   وَحُزْنًا طَوِيـلاً رَائِحًا ثُمَّ غَادِيَـا

وَنَادَى مُنَادِى الْحُبِّ أَيْنَ أَسِيرُنَـا   لَعَـلَّكَ مَـا تَــزْدَادُ إِلاَّ تَمَادِيَـا

حَمَلْتُ فُؤَادِى إِنْ تَعَلَّـقَ حُبَّهَـا   جَعَلْتُ لَهُ مِنْ زَفْرَةِ المَوْت فَادِيَا

___

I only want to travel

if the road takes me northward,

and I only like the lightning

if it strikes in Yemen!

For a woman like Leyla

any man would want to kill himself,

even if like me, he could accustom himself to despair.

If it is important to dream about peace and serenity,

then I want, O Leyla, to meet you all alone.

Weakness has taken its hold of my body

and a sadness subsists

from the morning until the evening.

Love's messenger calls:

"Where is the prisoner?

He persists always,

and always more and more!"

Oh! Much shall my heart endure

if it goes on loving.

Hold your breath, O death,

for love is my pledge![6]

(6)

مَنَعْتُ عن التسليم يــوم وَدَاعهـا   فودَّعْتُهـا بالطَّــرْفِ والعَيْـنُ تَدمَــعُ

وأُخْرِسْتُ عن رَدِّ الجواب فمن رأى   مُجِبًـا بدمـع العيـن قَلْبـا يُـــوَدَّعَ

علــيكِ سلامُ الله منـــى تحيُّـــــةً   إلى أن تغيب الشمس من حيث تطلعُ

───────────────

They forbade me to visit her

on the day that she traveled,

but my crying eyes

bade her farewell.

They forbade me to talk to her.

Oh, who has seen a lover in tears,

a heart that bids farewell?

"Oh, may you have God's protection

and my greeting,

right from the time that the sun rises

until it sets!"[7]

(7)

إذا نظرتْ نحوى تكلَّم طرفُها	وجاوبها طرفى ونحن سكـوتُ
فواحـــدة منهـــا تُــبَشِّرُ باللّقــا	وأُخرى لها نفسى تكـاد تموتُ
إذا متُّ خوفَ اليأْس أَحيانيَ الرّجا	فكـم مرَّةٍ قد متُّ ثم حَيِـــيت
ولوْ أُحْدَقوا بى الإنسُ والجِنُّ كلُّهم	لكى يمنعونى أن أجيك لجِـيت

If she looked my way

her eyes talked to me,

and then my eyes answered her back silently.

"We shall meet again".

Her eyes predict it,

but then in the same eyes

it is death that is waiting for me.

I fear, I despair,

I die and I live again through my hope.

How many times have I not been dead

and resuscitated?

They are all here around me,

men, *jinns,*

but I do not care!

If they think they can forbid me from seeing you:

I shall come to you anyway![8]

(8)

أشارتْ بعينيهـا مخافـة أهلهـا   إشارَة محـزونٍ بغيـر تَكلُّـم
فأيقنتُ أن الطرف قـد قـال مَرْحَبًـا   وأهـلاً وسهـلاً بالحبيـب المتيَّـم

She gave me a sign with her eyes

of fear of her parents,

- a sad sign,

which did not need any words -.

But I understood that her look

was telling me hello

and welcoming my orphaned soul.[9]

(9)

وما الناس إلا العاشقون ذوو الهـوى   ولا خيـر فيمـن لا يُـحبُّ ويَـعشقُ

إذا لُمْتُهـا قـالـتْ وعَـيْـنِيْكِ إننـا   حِراصٌ على اللُّقْيـا ولا نتفـرَّقُ

فإن كنتَ مشتاقـا فَسِرْ نحـو بابنـا   فنحن إلى ما كان مـن ذاك أشْوَقُ

———————————

The good persons

are only those who can love.

Nothing positive

can be created by someone

who neither can love

or be in love.

If I am reproachful to her,

she says: "I swear by your life,

I do not wish anything more

than that we reunite and never separate.

If you long for me,

then come to my door.

for I long for you

even more."[10]

(10)

فيا ليتنى لو كنت بعض برودِها | زهـا جسم ليلى فى الثيـاب تَنَعُّمًـا

رأيـتك يقظانًـا فعنـدى شُهُودهـا | أفى النـوم يا ليلى رأيـتك أم أنـا

فلـم تُطفَ نيرانى وزِيـد وَقودُهـا | ضممتك حتى قلت نارى قد انطفَت

———————————

Your whole body in its garment

is radiant in its beauty and gaiety, O Leyla.

Oh! How I wish that I could be revived

by its refreshing warmth!

I have seen you,

I have seen you,

- was it in my dreams -?

or with my loving eyes

in the light of the day?

I said holding you in my arms:

"My fire dies!"

But no, the fire does not die.

It still burns,

it is stronger![11]

إِلَى خُرَّدٍ لَيْسَتْ بِسُودٍ وَلاَ عُصْلِ	لَيَالِيَ أَصْبُو بِالْعَشِيِّ وَبِالضُّحَى
كَوَاعِبَ تَمْشِي مِشْيَةَ الْخَيْلِ فِى الْوَحْلِ	مُنَعَّمَةِ الأَطْرَافِ هِيفٍ بُطُونُهَا
وَأَعْيُنُهَا مِنْ أَعْيُنِ الْبَقَرِ النُّجْلِ	وَأَعْنَاقُهَا أَعْنَاقُ غِزْلاَنِ رَمْلَةِ
وَأَثْلاَثُهَا الْوُسْطَى كَثِيبٌ مِنَ الرَّمْلِ	وَأَثْلاَثُهَا السُّفْلَى بُرَادِيُّ سَاحِلِ
عَنَاقِيدُ تُغْذَى بِالدِّهَانِ وَبِالْغِسْلِ	وَأَثْلاَثُهَا الْعُلْيَا كَأَنَّ فُرُوعَهَا
وَأَطْرَافِهَا مَا تُحْسِنُ الرَّمْىَ بِالنَّبْلِ	وَتَرْمِى فَتَصْطَادُ الْقُلُوبَ عُيُونُهَا
صُبَابَاتِ مَاءِ الشَّوْقِ بِالأَعْيُنِ النُّجْلِ	زَرَعْنَ الْهَوَى فِى الْقَلْبِ ثُمَّ سَقَيْنَهُ
هِىَ النَّبْلُ رِيشَتْ بِالفُتُورِ وَبِالكُحْلِ	رَعَابِيبُ أَقْصَدْنَ الْقُلُوبَ وَإِنَّمَا
بِلاَ قَوَدٍ عِنْدَ الْحِسَانِ وَلاَ عَقْلِ	فَفِيمَ دِمَاءُ الْعَاشِقِينَ مُطَلَّةٌ
أَمَا فِى الْهَوَى يَارَبِّ مِنْ حَكَمٍ عَدْلِ	وَيَقْتُلْنَ أَبْنَاءَ الصَّبَابَةِ عَنْوَةً

When the night falls and the dawn breaks,

I dream of a pure and beautiful virgin, slender and tender,

with nice curves, thin waist and round breasts,

moving steadily like a mare on a muddy soil.

Her neck is the neck of the desert deer.

Her eyes remind of the buffalo's big eyes.

Her lower third part is strong as iron, glittering as a river.

Her middle third part is a sand dune.

Her upper third part is branches and bunches of grapes,

fragrant and filled with sweet juices.

Her eyes aim right and hit all the men's hearts:

no one can avoid their deadly arrows.

She has sown the seeds of love in my heart and watered them

with the water of longing that sleeps in her big eyes.

This terrified heart, you know well how to hit it,

O you the gracious and languishing arrow,

embellished by feathers and make-up.

Truly, the beautiful woman can make her lover's blood shed

without feeling any remorse or paying a price.

By God, she could kill violently the one who loves her

without fearing the law or the hand of justice,

for when did justice intervene

in the matters of love?[12]

(12)

هى الخمر فى حُسْنٍ وكالخمْرِ ريقُها　　ورقَّةُ ذاك اللونِ فى رقَّـة الخمْـر

وقد جُمِعَتْ منهـا خمـورٌ ثلاثـةٌ　　وفى واحد سُكْرٌ يَزيد على السُّكـرِ

———————————————

Her beauty is like wine,
her saliva and its clarity too.
Three kinds of wine
have mixed together in her,
one more intoxicating than the other.[13]

(13)

تَقُولُ لَنَا أَسْتَوْدِعُ اللهَ مَـنْ أَدْرِى	ومِمَّـا شَجَانِـى أَنَّهَـا يَـوم وَدَّعَت
وقد ضَاقَ بِالْكِتْمَانِ مِنْ حُبِّهَا صَدْرِى	وَكَيْـف أُعَزِّى النَّفْسَ بعـد فِرَاقِهَـا
لقد كادَ رُوحِى أَنْ يَزُولَ بِلاَ أَمْرِى	فَـــوَاللهِ واللهِ الْعَزِيـــــز مَكَانُـــــهُ
وقُولاَ لِلَيْلَى ذا قَتِيلٌ مِـنَ الهَجْـر	خَلِيلَـىَّ مُـرَّا بعـد مَوْتِـى بِتُرَبَتِـى

O the worst of misery!

Our farewell day.

"I know," she said,

"who I shall leave in the hands of God."

But can I now in my loneliness

silence my soul

when my loving heart

is not able to repress this love any more?

O God, my God,

my Almighty God,

my life leaves me,

she goes her way,

I cannot stop her.

When I disappear, my friends,

go to where I sleep,

and then say to Leyla:

"You have left him,

he is dead."[14]

(14)

أُحبُّك يـا ليلى وأُفرط فـى حَبِّــى   وتُبدين لى هجرا على البعد والقُرْبِ

وأهواك يا ليلى هـوّى لـو تـنسَّمت   نفوسُ الورى أدناه صِبْحنَ من الكَرب

شكـوت إليهـا الشوق سِرًّا وجهـرةً   وبحْتُ بمـا ألقـاه مـن شِدّة الـحُبِّ

ولمـا رأيتُ الصدَّ منها ولـم تكـن   تَرِقُّ لشكواتى شكوتُ إلى ربى

إذا كان قـرب الـدار يـورث حسرةً   فلا خير للصبّ المتيَّم فى القـرب

———————

I love you, O my Leyla,

I persist on loving you,

you, who near or far,

think only of avoiding me!

I love you, O my Leyla,

and the smallest sigh of this love,

carried away by the wind, inhaled,

would trigger a deep torment

in a passerby's soul.

Yes, I complain to her

about this longing,

in public and all alone.

All silently I tell her

about my heart's sorrow.

If I beg for her help,

she is deaf for my prayers,

then I pray to God.

What do I gain if I see her close to me?

Tears.

In love and entranced,

so terrible it is if she is near![15]

(15)

وَهَلَّلَ لِلرَّحْمـنِ حيـنَ رَآنـى	وأَجْـهَشْتُ لِلتَّوْبَـادِ حِيـنَ رَأَيْتُـهُ
ونادَى بأَعْلَى صَوْتِهِ ودَعَانِى	وأَذْرَيْتُ دَمْعَ الْعَيْـنِ لَمَّـا رَأَيْتُـهُ
حَوَالَيْكَ فى خِصْبٍ وطِيبِ زَمَانٍ	نَقُـلْتُ لـه أيـنَ الَّذِيـنَ عَهِدْتُهُـمْ
ومَنْ ذا الَّذى يَبْقَى مع الْحَدثَـانِ	فقَـالَ مَضَوْا وَاسْتوْدَعُونى بِلاَدَهُـمْ
فِـــرَاقُكِ وَالْحَيُّـــانِ مُؤْتَلِفَـانِ	وإنى لأَبْكِى الْيَوْمَ مِنْ حَـذرِى غَـدًا
وسَحًّا وتسْجَامًا إلى هَمَـلاَنِ	سِجَـالاً وتَهتانـا ووَبْـلاً ودِيمَـةً

When I saw the mountain of Tawbād,

my heart was seized by sorrow.

When it saw me

it invoked the Merciful.

When I recognized it

I started immediately to cry.

It called me with its highest voice.

"In your surroundings", I said, "I had friends.

It was the bright time, the happy one, the past."

"They are all gone", it said.

"It is now I who am guarding their land.

Who can fight Destiny?

Everything changes,

but you know that well."

Today I cry, and tomorrow?

I feel terrified.

Our tribes are now united,

but you shall also go your way.

O this water that richly flows out of its bowl,

heavy showers, storms, silent rains,

O tears![16]

(16)

أَمِنْ أجل خيماتٍ على مَذرَج الصَّبا   بجرعاءَ تعفوها الصَّبا والجَنائبُ

ألا قاتــل الله الركـــائبَ إنمـــا   تُفـرّق بيـن العاشقيـن الركـائبُ

بَكَـرْنَ بكـورًا واجتمعـن لموْعـدٍ   وسِار بقلبـى بينهـن النجـائبُ

———————————

Is it the camp's fault

that it is situated in the Orient

or a sand dune's

that an eastern or southern wind erases?

These horses,

Oh! I wish they were dead!

They can so well separate the lovers!

Trotting away since dawn

and always faithful to a meeting;

my heart's dearest part has left me

without leaving a trace![17]

(17)

أمـرُّ علــى الديـار ديـارِ ليلــى   أُقَبِّــل ذا الجــدارَ وذا الجـــدارَا

ومــا حبُّ الديـارِ شغَفـنَ قلبـى   ولكــنْ حبُّ مَـنْ سكـن الديــارَا

When I pass by the house,

Leyla's house,

I kiss its walls,

this one and that one.

"Is it of loving the walls

that you have lost your senses?"

"No, not the walls, my friend,

but the one who lives behind the walls!"[18]

(18)

ولـولا ذاك لا أُدعـى مصابـا	أبـوس تـراب رجـلك يا لويلـى
ولْكـنْ حبُّ مـن وطـىء التـرابـا	ومـا بَـوس التـراب لــحب أرض
محبًـا أستطـيب بهـا العذابـا	جُنـتُ بهـا وقد أصبـحت فيهـا
وعيـشى بالوحـوش نمـا وطابـا	ولازمْتُ القفـار بكــلّ أرض

Majnūn came to visit Leyla in the camp, but did not find her anywhere. He then started to kiss the earth.

I kiss the earth on which your foot has stepped,

O soft Leyla.

They say: "Look at the madman. See what he is doing!"

Do I love the earth so much

that I have to kiss it?

No! It is you that I love

and your steps on it.

It is you whom I am madly in love with.

It is because of you that I find comfort

in the memories that torment me.

For ever separated from the towns,

in the desert I must live,

hoping there to find some peace

among the beasts![19]

(19)

وما ذنبُ شاةٍ طبَّق الأرضَ ذيُها	أتُضرب ليلى كلما زرت دارها
مهينى وليلى سرُّ روحى وطيبها	فَمْكـرِمُ ليلى مُكرمـى ومُهينهـا
عليها لأجلى واستمـرَّ رقيبهـا	لئن منعـوا ليلى السلام وضيّقـوا
وطُفت بيوت الحَىِّ حيثُ أُصيبها	أتـيت ولـو أنَّ السـيـوف تَنوشنـى
وليت الذى تنوى لنا لا يصيبها	فليت الـذى أنـوى لليلى يُصيبنـى
هوى كل نفس أين حلَّ حبيبها	فلا تعذلونى فـى الخِطار بمهجتى

Must they hit Leyla every time

that I visit her dwelling?

Is it the lamb's fault

that the wolf is drawn to this enclosure!

The one who honors Leyla honors me,

the one who despises her despises me,

for truly, Leyla is my soul's happiness and goodness.

It is of no use to forbid Leyla to greet me,

to lock her in and to continuously spy on her,

as I shall not give her up

even if I must defy the brandished swords,

and I shall look for her in the whole camp

until I find her!

Alas! If the happy destiny

that I wish for Leyla, was mine!

Oh! May she never experience

the sad destiny that she has chosen for me!

Oh! Do not blame me if I put my life at risk:

The place of every soul is by its beloved.[20]

(20)

يقولون لى يومًا وقـد جئْتُ حَّيهُمْ   وفى باطنى نـارٌ يُشَبُّ لهيبُهــا

أمَا تختشى مـن أُسْدِنـا فأجبتُهـــمْ   هوى كل نفس أيّنَ حلّ حبيبُهـا

———————————

They asked me once when I came to visit their quarter

with a fire in my heart that was burning:

"Are you not afraid of our lions?"

And I answered:

"The place of every soul is by its beloved"![21]

(21)

أيا ليلى بكَى لى بعينيك رحمةً   من الوجد ، مما تعلمين ، وأعلَمُ

أليس عجيبا أن نكون ببلدة   كِلانـا بهـا يَشْقـى ولا نتكلَّـمُ

لئن كان ما ألقى من الحب أننى   بـه كَلِـفٌ جَـمُّ الصبابـةِ مُغـرمُ

لعـلك أن تَرثِـى لعَبْـدٍ مُتَيَّـمٍ   فمثـلك يـا ليلى يَـرِقُّ ويَرْحَـمُ

بكى لِىَ يا ليلى الضميـرُ وإنـه   ليبكى بمـا يلقـى الفـؤاد ويَعلـمُ

When Majnūn went to visit Leyla, her family forbade her to receive him. He cried then and recited these verses:

Both of us know, O Leyla,

that you have cried of compassion

and love over me.

Is it not strange that we both live in a country

in which we cannot more see each other

and in which we are in agony?

I have been afflicted by infatuation,

love and glowing passion.

You are probably mourning over an orphaned slave,

because a woman like you, O Leyla,

is compassionate and tender.

Reason, O Leyla,

has cried bitter tears over me,

when it knew about the hardships

that my heart was enduring.[22]

(22)

علــيّ ولكــن مــلءُ عَيْــن حبيبُهـا	أهــابك إجـــلالاً ومـــا بك قـــدرة
قليـلٌ ولكــن قــلَّ مـنكِ نصيُبهـا	ومـا هجرتُك النـفسُ أنك عندهـا
بقـول إذا مـا جـئْتُ : هذا حبيبها	ولكنهـم يـا أملـحَ النـاس أكثـروا
وما ذنبُ ليلى إنْ طوى الأرض ذِيُها	أتُضرَبُ ليلى إنْ مررْتُ بذى الغضى

I honor you and fear you.

Shall I defy your power?

No, you are the apple of my eye!

Shall I abandon you?

No, You live in my soul,

Leyla, you who gave me so little happiness!

O the kindest of people

who say every time they see me coming:

"Here comes Leyla's beloved!"

Shall they hit Leyla

every time that I pass by her dwelling?

Spare the innocent

when the wolf is drawn to this enclosure![23]

(23)

ألا هل طُلوعُ الشَّمْسِ يُهْدِى تَحِيَّـةً   إلـى آل لَيْلَـى مَـرَّةً أو غُرُوبُهــا

أتُضرَبُ لَيْلَى إنْ مَرَرْتُ بِذِى الغَضَى   وَمَا ذَنْبُ لَيْلَى إنْ طَوى الأرضَ ذيُها

أجَلْ وَعَلَىَّ الرَّجْـمُ إنْ قُـلْتُ حَبَّـذَا   غُـرُوبُ ثَنَايَـا أُمّ عَمْـرِو وَطِيهــا

You shall greet, O sun,

Leyla and her family.

But when? Tell me:

at dawn or when you set?

Why do they hit Leyla every time

when I pass by her dwelling?

It is not Leyla's fault

if the wolf is drawn to the enclosure.

But if your anger must be stilled,

stone me to death the day when I say:

"The wolf has gone away

with his sense of smell

and his cutting teeth!"[24]

(24)

مليحةٍ أطلال العشيّات لـو بـدت   لوْحشٍ شَرودٍ لاطمـأنّت قلوبُهـا

أهـابك إجـلالا ومـا بك قــدرة   علـىّ ولكـن مـلء عيـن حبيبُهـا

———————————

O the remains of the camp,

O the soft presence,

for the wandering wild man

when the evening falls!

When his heart sees them

it becomes filled with hope.

I honor you and fear you.

Shall I defy your power?

No. You are the apple of my eye![25]

(25)

يقولــون ليْلــى بالعِـــرَاقِ مَـــريضةٌ   فَمَــا لَكَ لا تَضنَــى وأنْتَ صَدِيــقُ

شَفَى اللهُ مَـرْضَى بالعِـراقِ فإنّـى   على كُلُّ مَرْضَى بالعِراقِ شَفِيـقُ

فـإِنْ تَكُ لَيْلَـى بالعِـراقِ مَـريضَةً   فإنّـيَ فِـى بحْـرِ الْخُـفوفِ غَريـقُ

أهِيــم بأقطــارِ البــلادِ وعَرْضِهَــا   ومَالِى إلى لَيْلَـى الغَـدَاةَ طَرِيـقُ

كأنَّ فُؤَادِى فيِهِ مُـورٍ بِقَـادِحٍ   وفيه لهيبٌ سَاطِـعٌ وَبُـرُوقُ

When Majnūn was asleep, a man woke him up and told him:

ألا إن ليلـــى بالعـــراق مـــــريضة   وأنت خَلـيُّ البـالِ ئلهـو وترقــدُ

"*Leyla is in Iraq and is sick,
how can you be lying down like this,
unaffected and asleep?*"

He then fainted, and when he awoke he recited these verses.

They say: "Leyla is in Iraq and is sick

How can you, who are her friend, be so unaffected?"

May God cure all the sick people in Iraq,

because I feel sorry for all the sick people there

If it is true that Leya is in Iraq and is sick

than the sea of death can hold me in its arms

and drown me!

Lost, I wander from place to place

and the morning closes again the path to Leyla,

Someone, I think, has lit a flame in my heart

which has spread and burst into bolts of lightning!

إذا ذَكَرَتها النـفْسُ مَاتَتْ صَبَابَةً   لَهَـا زَفـرَةٌ قَتّالــةٌ وشَهيــقُ

سَقَتنى شَمسٌ يُخْجِلُ البَدرَ نُورهُا   ويَكْسِفُ ضَوْءَ البَرْقِ وهْوَ بَـرُوقُ

غَرَابِيَّـةُ الْفَرْعَيْـنِ بَدرِيَّـةُ السنَـا   ومَنظَرهُا بَـادِى الْجَمَـالَ أنيـقُ

وَقد صِرْتُ مَجنُونًا مِنَ الْحُبّ هائمًا   كأنّـىَ عَـانٍ فى القُيُـودِ وَثِيـقُ

أظل رَزيحَ الْعَقْل مَا أطْعَمُ الكـرَى   وَللقـلْبِ مِنـى أنّـةٌ وخُفُـوقُ

بَرى حُبُّها جِسْمى وَقلْبى وَمُهْجَتى   فَلَـم يَبْـقَ إلا أعْظمٌ وَعُــرُوقُ

فلاَ تعْذِلُونى إن هَلَكْتُ تَرَحَّمُـوا   علىَّ فَفَقْـدُ الـرُّوحِ لـيْسَ يَعُـوقُ

وَخُطُّوا عَلَى قَبْرى إذَا مِتُّ واكْتُبـوا   قَتيـلُ لِحَـاظٍ مَـاتَ وَهـوَ عَشِيـقُ

إلَى اللهِ اشْكُو مَا أُلاقى مِنَ الْهـوَى   بِلَيْلَى فَفى قَلْبى جَـوًى وَحَريـقُ

With bitter tears and with a last wheeze,

my soul remembers you and dies of love.

I have delighted in a sun, which pulls the full moon to its shame,

and which conceals the lightning when it strikes.

Blacker than pitch are your locks

and clearer than the moon is your face.

O grace! O perfect beauty!

I have become madly in love and restless,

and I am suffering like a slave in chains!

My reason has weakened and sleep has left me.

All this is too unbearable for a heart

which pounds hard and cries.

Nothing more remains of me than bones and veins:

my love for her has destroyed my body, my heart and my soul.

If I die, do not blame me, but pity me:

a lost soul deserves that one cries over it.

Then write these words over my gravestone:

"It was eyes that killed him.

He is dead as a lover."

To God I complain

and ask for His Mercy.

I have loved and endured too much!

My heart continues to burn for Leyla.[26]

(26)

أقول لأصحابى هى الشمسُ ضوءُها   قـريبٌ ولكـن فـى تناولهـا بعْـدُ

لقـد عارضتنـا الريحُ منهـا بنفحــة   على كبدى من طِيب أرواحها بَـرْدُ

فمـا زلتُ مغشيًّا علىّ وقـد مَضَتْ   أنـاةٌ ومـا عنـدى جــوابٌ ولا رَدُّ

أُقــلَّبُ بالأيـدى وأهلـى بعَوْلَـةٍ   يُفَدُّونى لو يستطيعـون أن يَفـدُوا

———————

I say to my friends: "She is the sun.

Its light surrounds you

but it remains distant

and inaccessible to everyone!"

But the wind hit me right in the heart:

It was her breath.

O scent! O freshness!

The end comes now.

Unconscious and impatient,

all the words have left me.

They carry me,

they take me away,

I hear my relatives cry,

wanting to sacrifice their lives

if they only could rescue me! [27]

(27)

رُعَاةَ اللَّيْلِ ما فعلَ الصَّبَاحُ   وما فَعَلَتْ أَوائِلُهُ الْمِلاَحُ

وما بالُ الَّذِينَ سَبَوْا فُؤَادى   أَقَامُوا أَمْ أَجَدَّ بِهِمْ رَوَاحُ

وما بَالُ النُّجُومِ مُعَلَّقَاتٍ   بِقَلْبِ الصَّبِّ ليس لها بَرَاحُ

كَأَنَّ الْقَلْبَ لَيْلَةَ قِيلَ يُغْدَى   بِلَيْلَى الْعَامِرِيةِ أَوْ يُرَاحُ

قَطَاةٌ عَزَّهَا شَرَكٌ فَبَاتَتْ   تُجَاذِبُهُ وقد عَلِقَ الجَنَاحُ

When Majnūn was wandering around, he met a few shepherds who told him that Leyla's parents have taken her away to meet the man whom they chose for her to marry.

O night's shepherds,

see how the morning's first soft hours have weakened me!

Oh! What are they doing,

hose who have captivated my heart?

Have they pitched their camp somewhere,

or when the night has fallen,

have they moved away?

And why are these stars always hanging in the lovers' hearts?

"Tomorrow Leyla al-ᶜĀmirīya[28] shall go away

or maybe even tonight".

Oh these words in the night,

poor heart,

defeated heart,

like the grey partridge

in the net!

Courageously she fights,

but her wings are for ever caught.

لـهـا فَرْخـانِ قـد تُـرِكَـا بِقَفـرٍ وَعُشُّهُمَـا تُصَفِّقُـهُ الرِّيَـاحُ

إذا سَمِعَـا هُبُـوبَ الرِّيحِ هَبَّـا وقـالا أُمَّنـا ، تَأْتِـى الـرَّوَاحُ

فَـلا بِاللَّيْـلِ نَـالَتْ مَـا تُرَجِّـى ولا فى الصُّبْـحِ كـان لها بَـرَاحُ

رُعـاةَ اللَّيْـلِ كُونُـوا كَيْـفَ شِئْتُـمْ فقـد أَوْدَى بِـىَ الـحُبُّ المُتَـاحُ

––––––––––––

Her chicks are in the desert,

defenseless and abandoned.

The wind blows angrily

and overturns their nest.

When they hear it howling,

they shiver and call:

"O mother, it is time!

The evening is here. Return!"

But this hope disappears in the night,

there is no use,

and no help either comes in the morning.

O night's shepherds

live as you please.

I was already dead

when I could have loved![29]

(28)

ألاَ يا نَسيمَ الرِّيحِ حُكْمُكَ جائِرٌ   علــىَّ إذا أَرْضَيْتَنـــى وَرَضيت

ألاَ يا نَسيمَ الرِّيحِ لو أَنَّ واحِــدًا   منَ النَّاسِ يُبْليـه الهَوَى لَبَليتُ

فَلَوْ خلِطَ السَّمُ الزُّعَاف بِريقِهــا   تَـمَصَّصْت منـهُ نَهْلَــةً وَرَويتُ

You treat me so badly,

O soft breeze,

you who in the happy days

could bring me so much comfort!

If ever there is a man,

one only man in the whole world,

who is weary of love,

O breeze, it is I.

And if a deadly poison

mixed with her saliva, [30]

one only sip would suffice

to quench my thirst![31]

(29)

فَيَا قَلبُ مُتْ حُزْنًا وَلاَ تَكُ جَازِعَـا   فـإنَّ جَزُوعَ القَـوْمِ لَـيْسَ بِخَالِـدِ

هَـوِيتَ فتـاة نَيْلها الخُلدُ فالتَـــمس   سبيـلا إلى مـا لست يومـا بواجِــدِ

هَـوِيتَ فَـــاةً كَالْغَزَالَــةِ وَجْهُهَـــا   وَكَالشَّمْسِ يَسْبِى ذُلُّهَا كُلَّ عَابِدِ

وَلِى كَبِدٌ حَــرَّى وَقَــلْبٌ مُعَــذَّبٌ   وَدَمْعٌ حَثِيثٌ فى الهَوى غَيرُ جَامِدِ

وَآيَةُ وَجْـدِ الصَّبِّ تَهْطَالُ دَمْعِـهِ   وَدَمْعُ الشَّجِىِّ الصَّبِّ أَعْدَلُ شَاهِدِ

على مَا انْطَوَى مِنْ وَجْدِهِ فى ضَميرِه   على الآنِسَاتِ النَّاعِمَات الخَرَائِدِ

Do not suffer, O loving heart,

but rather die quickly filled with sorrow.

Our torments in this world always have an end.

You love a woman

whom only Eternity can give you

Go, strive,

try to find a path

to the one who, day after day,

must here avoid you.

You love a woman

whose face resembles a deer's,

and whose beauty, like the sun's,

draws to it men's adoring eyes.

Your soul is burning,

and your heart is tormented,

and of love for her

your tears have become incessant.

Yes, your crying is the best witness

of the true love that you feel

for such a soft and pure maiden.

فَيَا لَيْتَ أَنَّ الدَّهْرَ جَادَ بِرَجْعَةٍ   وَهَيْهَاتَ إِنَّ الدَّهْرَ لَيْسَ بِعَائِدِ

إِلَيْكَ فَعَزِّ النَّفْسَ واسْتَشْعِرِ الْأَسَى   فَحُبُّكَ يَنْمِي زَائِدًا غَيْرَ بَائِدِ

وَقَدْ شَسَعَتْ لَيْلَى وَشَطَّ مَزَارُهَا   وَغَيَّرَهَا عَنْ عَهْدِهَا قَوْلُ حَاسِدِ

فَيَا أَسَفَا حَتَّامَ قَلْبِي مُعَذَّبٌ   إِلَى اللهِ أَشْكُو طُولَ هٰذِي الشَّدَائِدِ

If only the happy days could return!

But Alas! Who has ever seen them returning?

Come! Find consolation, be strong,

as time does not kill but strengthen your love.

Shall I ever see Leyla again?

She is far, so far away!

The words of the envious have poisoned her soul.

How much longer shall you suffer, O tormented heart?

To God I complain about all these hardships,

and beg for His Mercy![32]

(30)

أُفَكِّرُ مـا ذَنْبِى إِلـيكِ فَأعْـجَبُ	مـوالله ثـمَّ والله إنَّـــى لَـــدَائِبٌ
وَأَىُّ أُمُورِى فِيكِ يَـا لَيْـلَ أرْكبُ	واللهِ مـا أدْرِى عَـــلاَمَ هَجَرْتِنِــــى
أمْ آشرَبُ كأْسَامِنكُمُ ليس يُشْرَبُ	أَأَقطَعُ حَبْلَ الْوَصْل ، فالموتُ دُونَه
أمْ آفعَلُ مـاذا ؟ أمْ أبُوحُ فَأُغْلَبُ	أمْ آهْرُبُ حتَّى لا أرَى لِى مُجَـاوِرًا
فَأوَّلُ مَهْجُـورٌ ، وَآخَرُ مُعْـتَبُ	فَأيُّهُمَـا يَـا لَيْـلَ مَـا تَفْعَلِينَـــهُ

Help me, O my God, I think of her all the time!

Leyla! What crime have I committed?

I am completely confused!

Why have you abandoned me?

My God! I do not know!

And what have I done to you?

Leyla, tell me about it!

Shall we not meet any more?

Death is then milder!

Shall I empty the glass from which no one drinks?

Or shall I flee far away,

farther away,

without anyone by my side?

Or what shall I do?

Shall I reveal this secret?

Then I shall be lost.

Leyla is confused in her relation to me:

a man whom one avoids,

a man whom one slanders.

فلــوْ تلْتَقِــى أرْوَاحُنَـا بَعْـد مَوْتِنَـا

ومَن دُونِ رَمْسَينا مِنَ الأرضِ مَنْكِبُ

لظَلَّ صَدَى رَمْسِى وإنْ كُنْتُ رِمَّـةً   لصَوْتِ صَدَى لَيْلَى يَهَشُّ ويَطربُ

ولـو أنَّ عينًـا طاوعتنِـيَ لــم تــزَلْ   تَرَقرَقُ دَمْعًا أو دمًا حيــن تَسْكُب

─────────

But if after our death our souls would unite?

The earth's surface can in vain heighten[33]

to hide our coffins from each other,

my soul, outside of my decomposed bones,

shall like a bird fly to meet your soul.[34]

Yes, my uninhibited soul, O Leyla,

shall celebrate and rejoice

when it shall listen to your voice![35]

And I shall say to my eyes: "Cry,

cry endlessly!

Shed tears or blod!"[36]

(31)

أمُــوت إذا شَطَّتْ وَأَحْيَــا إذا دَنَتْ   وَتَبْعَثُ أَحْزَانِى الصَّبَا وَنسِيمهَـا

فَمِنْ أَجْلِ لَيْلَى تُولَعُ العَيْنُ بِالْبُكَا   وَتَأْوِى إلَى نَفْسٍ كَثِيرٍ هُمُومهَـا

كأنَّ الْحَشَا مِن تَحْتِهِ عَلِقَتْ بِـه   يَدٌ ذَات أظْفَارٍ فَتَدْمى كلومُهَـا

I die if she goes away,

I live if she comes near.

The eastern wind revives my heart's torments.

And my eyes for Leyla can only cry

She lives in this soul devoured by worries.

One hand, I believe,

holds my heart captive,

under nails covered with blood,

penetrating and hurting.[37]

(32)

أمــا والــذى أرّسَى ثَبيــرا مكانـــه   عليه السّحــابُ فوقــه يتـنصَّبُ

وما سلك الموماةَ مـن كـلِّ حَسْرةٍ

لقـد عِشْتُ مـن ليلى زمانًا أُحِبُّهـا   طَليحٍ كجَفنِ السيف تَهْوِى فترْكَبُ

أخا الموت إذ بعضُ المحبين يَكذبُ

———————————

I swear by Him

Who chose to live

over the Thabīr mountain[38]

where the clouds gather together!

By the tired and haggard camel,

which angrily speeds

through the dry desert!

That Leyla, since a long time

I love her,

she is my life

or my death.

- Other lovers can tell lies -.[39]

(33)

وَجَدْتُ الْـحُبَّ نيرانًا تَلَظّـى   قُلـوبُ الْعَاشِقِيـنَ لَهَـا وَقـودُ

فَلـوْ كـانَتْ إذَا احْتَـرَقَتْ تفـانَتْ   وَلكِـنْ كُلَّمَـا احْتَـرَقَتْ تَعُـودُ

كأهْـل النَّـار إذْ نضِجَتْ جُلُـودٌ   أُعِيدَتْ ــ لِلشَّقَاءِ ــ لَهُمْ جُلـودُ

———————

Love, I see it well,

is a glowing fire,

and of the lovers' hearts

it nourishes itself.

If only when they were burnt

they could finally die!

But alas! As soon as they have turned to ashes

they resuscitate, like the damned:[40]

their transformed skin,

again and again, restores itself

for new torments.[41]

(34)

بِنَفْسِىَ مَنْ لَابُدَّ لِى أَنْ أُهَاجِـرُهْ	وَمَنْ أَنَا فِى المَيسُورِ وَالْعُسْرِ ذَاكِرُهْ
وَمَنْ قَدْ رَمَاهُ النَّاسُ بِى فَاتَّقَاهُـمُ	بِهَجْـرِىَ إِلاَّ مَـا تُجِـنُّ ضَمَائِـرُهْ
فَمِنْ أَجْلِهَا ضَاقَتْ عَلَىَّ بِرُحْبِهَـا	بِـلاَدِىَ إذْ لـم أُرْضَ عَمَّنْ أُجَـاوِرُهْ
وَمِنْ أَجْلِهَا أَحْبَبْتُ مَنْ لاَ يُحِبُّنِـى	وَباغَضْتُ مَنْ قَدْ كُنْتُ حِينًا أُعَاشِرهْ
أَتَهْجُـرُ بَيْتًـا لِلْحَبِـيبِ تَعَلَّـقَتْ	بِهِ الْحِبُّ والأعداء أَمْ أَنْتَ زَائِرُهْ

She whom I ought to forget,

lives in my soul.

Whether I am glad or sad,

she occupies all my thoughts.

The evil people destroy her

with their slanders about me.

She fears them all

and drives me away,

except from her heart.

My country's wide horizons

have become narrow;

I have no friend

in whom I can delight in,

it is all Leylas fault.

For her sake I have loved

those who did not love me

and broken the ties

with those who did.

The loved one, the camp:

here is love,

here are the enemies.

Will you flee?

Will you visit her?

وَكَيْفَ خَلاصِي مِنْ جَوَى الْحُبِّ بَعْدَما

وقد مَاتَ قَبْلِى أَوَّلُ الْحُبِّ فَانْقَضَى   يُسَرُّ بِهِ بَطْنُ الْفُؤَادِ وَظَاهِرُهْ

وقد كان قَلْبِى فى حِجَابٍ يَكُنُّهُ   فإن مِتُّ أضْحَى الْحُبُّ قد مَات آخِرُهْ

أصُدُّ حَياءً أَنْ يَلِحَّ بِىَ الْهَوَى   فَحُبُّكِ مِنْ دُونِ الْحِجَابِ يُبَاشِرُه

                                        وفيك المُنَى لولا عَدُوٌّ أُحَاوِرُهْ

———————

How shall I free myself

from love's hidden torments

when they have become my heart's joys

and its only choice?

The time of falling in love has died

before I have awaken,

but if I must die,

the mature love dies at the same time.

I have hidden my heart in vain

behind a veil,

my passion for you has torn the veil

and seized the heart.

My honor complains

over such a demanding love,

but you are the gift

or the enemy to fear.[42]

(35)

فآشكوهـا غرامـى والتهابـى	يميل بِىَ الهـوى فى أَرْض ليلـى
وقلبى فى همـوم واكتئـاب	وأُمْطِرُ فى التراب سحـاب جفنى
ودمعى فى انهمـال وانسيـاب	وأشكو للديار عظيـم وجـدى
كأن التـرب مُستمـع خطابى	أُكلّم صورة فـى التـرب منهـا
مصابى والحديثُ إلى التـراب	كأنى عندهـا أشكـو إليهـا
ولا العتّاب يَرْجع فى جوابى	فـلا شخصٌ يـرد جـواب قولى
هَتُونٌ مثل تَسْكاب السحـاب	فأرجـع خائبـا والدمـعُ منـى
وتلبى من هواهـا فـى عـذاب	على أنى بهـا المجنـون حقُّـا

To Leyla's country passion takes me.

I want to reproach her the love that tortures me.

My eyelids are clouds,

which pour down their rain upon the earth,

and my heart is devoured by worries and pains.

I reveal to the camp my excessive sorrow,

and like streams my tears flow without restraint.

I draw you in the sand, I talk to your picture,

Is it possible that the earth hears my prayers?

I imagine myself being close to you,

But alas! This speech and my pain's cry go only to the earth.

No one says anything; it is completely silent around me.

The one to whom I complain remains mute.

My tears, when I have lost my hope,

fall down like the rain out of the clouds.

Mad about you and because of you,

I am the madman, I know,

and my heart of loving you

only suffers and burns.[43]

(36)

ألاَ أيُّهــا الــقُصَّاد نحــوى لتعلمــوا

بحالى وما أصبحت فى القَفـر أصنــعُ

ألــم تعلمــوا أنَّ القَطــا قــد ألِفْتُـــه

وأن وُحــوش القفـر حولِــىَ تُرْئَــعُ

وعَــيشِكِ مــا لــى حيلــة غيـر أننــى

بِلَفْظِ الحصا والخطُّ فى الأرض مُولـعُ

إنَ وحــوش البَــرِّ يأتلفــون بــى

ذكــورٌ إنــاثٌ ثــم خشْفٌ ومُــرْضَع

دون مُقامــى فــى الفــلاة ووحدتــى

وعشقــى لليلــى لِلهمــوم تَجَمُّــعُ

O you who are persecuting me,

learn something about my life,

how in the desert

I spend my days.

I have tamed the grey partridge,

and the desert's wild animals

are grazing around me.

I swear by your life,

what can I do better, every day,

than to draw you in the sand,

and rejoice about the language of the stones?[44]

I have also gained the wild animals' friendship.

Wild? Not for me,

whether they are males, females,

first-borns or suckles.

I shall not talk about the cruel loneliness,

about my life in the desert,

about my passion for her;

O gathered pains that keep on haunting me![45]

(37)

وإنكِ لــو بلَّغتَهـا قولـــيَ اسْلمــــى
طَوَتْ حَزَنًا وارفَضَّ منها دموعُهـا

وَبَانَ الذى تُخفى من الشوق فى الـحَشى
إذا هاجهـا مِنِّـى حــديثٌ يُروعُهـا

وفاضتْ فلم تَملك سوى فَيْضٍ عَبْـرَةٍ
وقـلَّ لباقى العيشِ منهـا قُنُوعُهـا

إذا طلـــعت شمسُ النهـــار فسلمـــى
فآيــــة تسليمـــى علـــيك طلوعها

بـــعشرِ تحَيَـــــاتٍ إذَا الشمس أشرقت
وعشرٍ إذا اصفرَّت وحـان وقوعهـا

_____

If you send her my greeting, O friend,

she will, devastated by sorrow,

break out into tears,

and the concealed love in her troubled heart

will reveal itself by one only word from me.

And against her will she will then cry rivers,

and nothing in the world will gladden her any more.

Here comes the day!

The sun is rising! I send you my greeting!

You will recognize it by this sign: the dawn!

Ten times I greet you when the sun rises,

ten times when it shines,

and ten times too when it sets![46]

(38)

أظـــن هواهـــا تاركـــى بِمَضَلّـــةٍ   مِن الأرضِ لا مالٌ لدىَّ ولا أَهْـلُ

ولا أَحَـــدٌ أُفضِى إليـــهِ وَصِيَّتــــى   ولا صاحبٌ إلاَّ المطيَّةُ والرَّحْلُ

مَحَا حُبُّها حُبَّ الأُلَى كُنَّ قبلهـــا   وَحَلَّتْ مكانًا لم يَكُن حُلَّ مِنْ قَبْلُ

فحُبِّى لها حُبٌّ تمكَّن فى الــحشَا   فما إنْ أرى حُبًّا يكونُ له مِثْلُ

My love for her, I believe, forces me to wander

in a foreign country, all alone and poor.

I have no friend in whom I can confide in.

For company I have my camel mare and its saddle.

My love for her has made me forget

all those whom I have loved before.

She occupies a unique place

that no one else has occupied before her!

My passion for her dwells in my heart.

No other feeling, I know, can replace it.[47]

(39)

ألاَ أيُّها القلبُ الـذى لـجَّ هائمًـا   بليلى وَليدًا لـم تَقَطَّـعْ تَمَائِمـهْ

أفِق قد أفـاقَ العاشقون وقـد أنـى   لك اليوم أن تلقى طبيبا تلائمُـه

فمـالك مسلـوب العَـزَاءِ كأنمـا   ترى نأَى ليلى مَغْرَمًا أنت غارِمُة

أجَـدَّك لا تُـنْسِيك ليلـى مُلِمَّـةٌ   تُلِـمُّ ولا عهـدٌ يطـول تقادُمُـهْ

_____

Poor crazy heart in its love for Leyla,

a child whose amulet has not yet been removed![48]

You must get cured.

Lovers always get cured.

The time has now come for you

to find a good doctor.

Why are you so inconsolable,

and if Leyla is so far away,

why do you feel as though

you are indebted to her

and must immediately pay her back your debt?

Is it reasonable

that neither all your misfortunes,

nor the anticipated and always postponed moment,

that nothing can make you forget her?[49]

(40)

ألاَ يـا غـراب البيْـن لـــونك شـاحبٌ   وأنت بلوْعـــات الفــراق جديـــرُ

فبينْ لنا ما ما قلتَ إذْ أنت واقـع   وبيِّنْ لنـا مـا قـلتَ حيــن تطيــرُ

فإنْ يك حقًّا مـا تقـول فأصبــحتْ   همومُك شتَّى والجنـاحُ كسيـرُ

ولا زلت مطـرودًا عديمـا لنـاصـرٍ   كمـا ليس لـى مـن ظَالِمـىَّ نصيـرُ

O you crow,[50]

bird of absence,

your gloomy color

reminds me so well of the farewell's torments!

Let me know!

What do you say when you're resting?

Let me know!

What do you say when you're flying?

If your tales are true

then your sorrows are probably endless

and your wings are broken.

No one saves you

and you are always hunted,

like me, no one helps me

against those who oppress me.[51]

(41)

أقـول لِمُـفْتٍ ذاتَ يــوم لقيتُـه   بمكَّــةَ والأنضاء مُلْقــى رِحالهــا

بــرَبِّكَ أخبرنـى أَلَــمْ تأثـمِ التــى   أضرَّ بجسمى مـن زمـانٍ خيالُهــا

فقــال بلــى واللهِ سوف يَمَسُّهــا   عـذابٌ ، وبَلْـوَى فى الحيـاة تنالُها

فقـلت ولـم أمـلك سوابـقَ عَبْـرَةٍ   سَرِيع إلى جيب القميص انهمالها :

عفـا الله عنهـا ذنْبهـا وأقالهــا   وإن كـان فى الدنيـا قليـلاً نوالُهــا

I asked a mufti whom I met on that day,

it was in Mecca,

we had taken away the saddles

from our exhausted horses:

"Tell me, by God, she whose memory

incessantly consumes my body,

will she be forgiven?

He answered: "Never.

Torments, by God, will fall upon her.

She will experience misery!"

I could not stop myself from breaking out into tears,

which ran down on my shirt's collar.

"O! May God forgive her her sins," I said.

"Forget, O God, that in this world she gave so little!"[52]

(42)

وداع دعا إذ نحن بالخَيْفِ من مِنًى	فَهيَّجَ أحزانَ الفؤاد وما يَـدْرِى
دع بـاسم ليلَـى غيرهـا فكأنمـا	أطارَ بليلى طائرًا كانَ فى صدرِى
دعا بـاسم لَيْلى أسخـن الله عِينَـه	ولَيْلَى بأرضِ الشَّامِ فى بَلَدٍ قَفْـر
عرضتُ على قلبى العزَاء فقال لِى	مِنَ الآنَ فاجزَعْ لاَ تملَّ مِنَ الصبَّرِ
إذا بانَ من تهوَى وشَطَّ به النَّوى	فَفُرقة مَنْ تهوى أحرّ مـنَ الجمـر

When Majnūn was in al-Khayf, he heard someone call the name "Leyla", which made him faint. His family gathered around him and his father cried of sorrow. When he woke up, he recited these verses.

We were in Minā,[53] in al-Khayf.[54]

A man shouted out a name, reviving my soul's torments

without knowing it.

This call, it was Leyla's name... - without Leyla -,

and I felt as though a bird flew out from my heart.

Someone called: "Leyla"

Oh, May God tire out his eyes!

As Leyla is in Damascus,

in the desert, in which places?

I tell my heart to be patient, and it says:

"Be worried from this day, but you must endure!

When your beloved is far away,

deported and fleeing,

your passion for her

burns more than glowing coal!"[55]

(43)

حججتُ ولم أُحجِجْ لـذنبٍ جَنَيْتُهُ   ولكنْ لِتُعْدِى لى على قَاطعِ الحبْل

ذَهبْتَ بعقلى فى هواهـا صغيـرةً   وقـد كِبـرتْ سِنِّى فَرُدُّ بهـا عقلـى

وإلاَّ فَسَاوِ الـــحب بيـنـى وبينهـــا   فإنك يا مولاَى تحكُـمُ بالعَــذْل

───────────────

I did not beg during this pilgrimage

to make amends for a sin that I have committed,

but to receive assistance in renewing an old tie.

You have made me love her already as a young man

and you have made me fall madly in love with her.

Today I have become older.

So give me through her my reason back

or do so that the love between me and her

becomes mutual;

for You are know to be Just,

O my Merciful Lord,

in all Your deeds.[56]

(44)

ذَكرتُكِ والحجيجُ لهمْ ضجيـجٌ   بمكّةَ والقلوبُ لهـا وَجـيب

فقلتُ ونحـن فى بَلدٍ حرامٍ   بـه واللهُ أُخـلِصَتِ القلُـوب

أتوبُ إليكَ يا رحمـنُ ممـــا   عملتُ فقد تظاهرت الذُّنوبُ

فأمّا مِنْ هـوَى ليلَـى وتْركـى   زيارتَهـــا فإنــــى لا أتـــوب

وكيف ــ وعندها قلبى رهينٌ ــ   أتوبُ إلـيك منهـا أو أُنـيب ؟

———————————

During the pilgrim's days, Majnūn's father led him to a gathering of people and begged them to pray for him. When they started to pray, Majnūn recited these verses.

The pilgrims gather around me.

In Mecca one only heart pounds.

In this noise, among all these people,

my glowing thoughts go to you.

I have said in this holy place

in which our souls are pure and devoted to God:

"I am coming here, my Lord,

regretful and repenting all my sins,

Alas! All very obvious.

But about my love for Leyla,

if it is necessary that I do not visit her any more,

I cannot promise You that.

How can I do this?

My heart is her pledge.

To obey You or to be punished?

To abandon her for You? [57]

(45)

ذكرتك حيث استأمن الوحش والتقت

رفاق من الآفاق شتَّى شعوبُها

وعند الحَطيم قد ذكرتُك ذكرة

أرى أن نفسى سوف يأتيكِ حُوبُها

دعــا المُحرِمــون الله يستغفرونــه

بمكةَ شُعْثًا كى تُمَحَّى ذنوبُها

ناديتُ يا رحمنُ ، أولُ سُؤْلتــى

لنفسىَ لَيْلَى ثُمَّ أنتَ حَسِيبُهـا

وإن أُعطَ ليلى فى حياتَى لـم يَـتُبْ

إلـى الله عبــدٌ تَوْبَـةً لا أتوبُهــا

يقـرُّ بعينــى قُرْبُهــا ويزيدُنِــى

بها عَجَبًا مَن كان عندى يَعِيبُها

وكم قائلٍ قد قال تب فعصَيْتُـه

وتـلك لعمرى خَلَّةٌ لا أُصِيبُهـا

وما هجرتُكِ النفسُ يا ليَل أنَّهـا

قَلَتْكِ ولكِنْ قَلَّ مِنْك نصِيبُها

فيا نفسُ صبرًا لستِ واللهِ فاعلمـى

بأوَّلِ نفس غابَ عنها حبيبها

In this place in which the beasts are safe,[58]

and in which all the people, - united horizons -, become one.

By al-Ḥaṭīm[59] I have thought of you so much

that I felt that my soul was carrying its sorrow to you.

In Mecca, the pilgrim with uncombed hair,

is praying to God for His Mercy,

so that Leyla's sins become forgiven.

I have called: "O Merciful, listen to me!

First You must give me Leyla, and then You can judge her!

If I have Leyla in this life,

then there will not be any man who will repent for his sin

unless that with him I shall repent for the same sin."

When she is close to me she is the apple of my eye,

I love her even more when she is criticized.

They tell me again and again: "Think of God!", but I refuse

because I swear she is a need that I will not repent for.

My soul has never hated you to ever want to abandon you,

O Leyla, you who have given me so little happiness!

Come, be patient, O my heart! You know it well:

you are not the first one

who has been separated from its beloved![60]

(46)

سَبِيلَ الصَّبَا يَخْلُصْ إِلَى نَسِيمُها	أَيا جَبَلَىْ نَعْمانَ بِاللهِ خَلِّيا
على كَبِدٍ لَمْ يَبْقَ إِلاَّ صَمِيمُهَا	أَجِدْ بَرْدَهَا أَوْ تَشْفِ مِنِّى حَرَارَةٌ
على نَفْسِ مَحْزُونٍ تَجَلَّتْ هُمُومُهَا	فَإِنَّ الصَّبَا ريحٌ إذا مَا تَـنَسَّمَتْ
وإذ نَحْنُ تُرضِيهَا بِـدَارٍ نُقِيمُها	لَيَالِـىَ أَهْلُونَـا بِنَعْمَـانَ جِيـرَةٌ
أَباقِيَةٌ أَم قـد تَعَـفَّتْ رُسُومُها	ويا ريـحُ مُـرّى بالديـار فخبِّـرى
وَأَقْتَـلُ دَاءِ الْعَاشِقِيـنَ قَدِيمُهَـا	أَلاَ إِنَّ أَدْوَائِـى بِلَيْلَـى قديمَـــةٌ
وَلَذَّةَ عَيْشٍ قد تَوَلَّى نَعِيمُهَا	تَذَكَّرْتُ وَصْلَ النَّاعِجِيَّاتِ بالضُّحَى
فَأَسْجَمَ غَرْبَاهَا فَطَال سجومُها	وَأَنتِ التِى هَيَّـجْتِ عَينِى بِالْبُكَـا
قَذَاها وقد يَأْتِى على الْعَيْن شُومُها	وقد قَذِيَتْ عَيْنى بِلَيْلَى وأُتْبِعَتْ
على كَبِدٍ لـم يَبْقَ إِلاَّ رَمِيمُهـا	خَلِيلَـىَّ قُومَـا بِالْعِصَابَـةِ فاعْصِبَـا

O Naᶜmān's[61] two mountains, by God you must allow

this wind to send its breeze to me!

May my heart be consoled and its sickness cured

by a fresh breath that can revive me!

The one who inhales the soft eastern wind

can appease the torments in his anguished soul.

Naᶜmān, during long days, has welcomed our tribes.

We embellished these places when we pitched our camps there!

O wind, blow, pass by the camp and tell me

whether its traces are still visible or whether they are erased.

The sickness which has afflicted me, O Leyla, is so old!

But if love's torments have lasted so long

they can only be more devastating!

I remember well our meetings in the mornings

when a white camel mare carried me forth to you.

How beautiful life was then,

happiness did not know any sorrow!

The reason why these tears are weakening my sight,

it is Leyla. It is for her that one sees them pouring so,

and the wound in my eyes that never heals.

O my friends, dress this bleeding heart,

which soon shall be reduced into ashes![62]

(47)

متى يشتفى مِنكِ الفؤادُ الْمُعَـذَّبُ   وسَهْمُ المنايا من وصالِكِ أُقْـرَبُ

فَبُعْـدٌ ووَجْـدٌ واشتيـاقٌ ورَجْفَـةٌ   فـلا أنتِ تُدنينـى ولا أنـا أُقْـرَب

كَعصفورةٍ فى كَفِّ طِفْلٍ يَرُمُّهَـا   تذوقُ حياض الموتِ والطفلُ يلْعبُ

فلا الطفلُ ذو عقْلٍ يَرِق لمـا بهـا   ولا الطيرُ ذو ريشٍ يطير فيـذهب

ولى ألْفُ وجْهٍ قد عـرفتُ طريقـه   ولكنْ بلا قلب إلى أيـن أذهبُ

_____

When shall my tormented heart
ever be healed from you?
Death stretches its arrow,
it is hurrying.
It will reach me before I see you again.
Separation, love, longing, despair!
Neither you come to me
and nor I go to you.
My destiny is like the destiny of a bird
in a little girl's hand:
she presses it hard
and makes it taste of the cup of death.
But the girl is playing
and does not care for her victim:
she is too young to pity it,
and the bird is too weak to fly away.
Of course that I know about thousands of places
to where I can lead my steps,
but where shall I go to, my heart,
if you are not with me?[63]

(48)

أَمَا تَرَى الْجِسْمَ قد أَوْدَى به الْعَطَبُ   إلـــيكَ عنّـــى هائـــــمٌ وَصِبْ

حَرُّ الصَّبابةِ والأَوْجاعُ والـوَصَبُ   لِلّهِ قلبِـــيَ مـــاذا قـــد أُتِيــحَ لـــهُ

  ضاقتْ عَلَيَّ بِلاَدُ اللهِ مَا رَحُبَتْ

يَا لَلرِّجالِ فهلْ فى الأَرضْ مُضطَرَبُ   الْبَيْنُ يُؤْلِمُنِى ، وَالشَّوْقُ يَجْرَحُنِى

وَالدَّارُ نازِحَةٌ وَالشَّمْلُ مُـنْشَعِبُ   كيف السَّبيلُ إلى ليلى وقد حُجِبَتْ

عَهْدِى بها زمَنًا مـا دُونَهَا حُـجُبُ

Abandon me to my crazy wandering!

Don't you see that this weakened body

is going to its death?

My poor heart!

It has endured too much in this earth:

passion's glow, defeat and torments!

God's big country has become too little for me:

O my friends, who shall ever find

for the confused man a secure place in this world?

Our separation pains me,

the longing tortures me:

they are so far away the places where she lives

and our reunion has now become impossible!

Where is the road that leads to Leyla?

Are they hiding her for me now,

- me who have never encountered

an obstacle on this path before? -[64]

(49)

حـلالٌ لليلى شتمُنـا وانتقاصُنـا   هنيئًـا ومغفـور لليلـى ذنوبُهـا

وما هجرتُك النفسُ يا ليَ عن قِلًى   قَلَتْك ولكـن قلًّ مـنك نصيبهـا

ولكنهم يا أحسنَ الناسِ أُكثـروا   بقولٍ إذا مـا جئتُ هـذا حبيُبهـا

يقـرّ بعينـى قربُهـا ويزيدنـى   بها كلَفًا من كان عنـدى يَعيبهـا

وكم قائلٍ قـد قال تُبْ فعصيتـه   وتلك لعمـرى توبـةٌ لا أتوبهـا

What slanders are poisoning Leyla's soul?

Is she thinking of me?

I forgive her her injustice.

Never has my heart hated you

to want to abandon you, O Leyla,

you who have given me so little happiness!

O how many times do the kindest persons

exclaim when they see me coming:

"Here comes Leyla's worshiper!"

When she is close to me

she is the apple of my eye.

I love her even more

when she is criticized.

They tell me again and again:

"Think of God", but I refuse,

for I swear she is a need

that I will not repent for![65]

(50)

وَأَنْتِ الَّتِى كَلَّفْتِنِى دَلَــجَ السُّرَى	وَجُونُ الْقَطَا بِالْجِلْهَتَيْنِ جُثُـومُ
وَأَنْتِ الَّتِى قَطَّعْتِ قَلْبِى حَــزَازَةً	وَرَقَّرَقْتِ دَمْعَ الْعَيْنِ فَهْىَ سَجُومُ
وَأَنْتِ الَّتِى أَغْضَبْتِ قَوْمِى فَكُلُّهُمْ	بَعِيد الرِّضى دَانى الصُّدُود كَظِيمْ
وَأَنْتِ الَّتِى أَخْلَفْتِنِى مَا وَعَدْتِنِى	وَأَشْمَتِّ بِى مَنْ كَانَ فِيكِ يَلُـوم
وَأَبْرَزْتِنِى لِلنَّـاسِ ثُـمَّ تَرَكْتِنِى	لَهُـمْ غَرَضًا أُرْمَى وَأَنْتِ سَلِيمْ
فَلَوْ أَنَّ قَوْلاً يَكْلِمُ الْجِسْمَ قَدْ بَــدَا	بِجِسْمِىَ مِنْ قَوْلِ الْوُشَاة كُلُومُ

Oh you who have forced me

to take a journey in the night,

at the time when the grey partridge

sleeps over Jilhatān.[66]

You who have angrily broken my heart.

You for whom I have cried rivers!

You who have turned all my people against me,

all of them indignant, furious,

driving me away with their resentment!

You who have not kept your promises.

You who have turned me

into a laughing-stock and into a scapegoat

before all those who yesterday were slandering you!

You who have pointed at me

and threw me as a victim,

all alone before the slanderers' words

without paying for your crimes!

Oh! If the slanders could mark a body,

I would fear very much

that on my body one could read all these words![67]

(51)

فى حب من لا تَرى فى نَيْله طَمَعَا	مـا بالُ قَلبك يا مجنونُ قـد خُلِعَـا
فأَصبَحَا فى فُؤادى ثابتَيْـن مَعَـا	الـحب والـودُّ نِيطـا بالفـؤاد لهـا
لقد نَفى اللهُ عنـهُ الهَـمَّ والجزعَـا	طُوبَى لمـن أنتِ فى الدنيا قرينتُـه
إلاّ ترقـرقَ مـاءُ العَيْـن أو دمعَـا	بـل مَا قَرأتُ كِتابًا مِنْكِ يَبْلُغُنِـى
حَتّى إذا قلتُ هـذا صادقٌ نَزعا	أدعـو إلى هجرهـا قلبى فيتبعنـى

لا أستطيـعُ نُزوعـا عـن مَوَدَّتِهَـا

ويَصنَعُ الحُبّ بى فوق الـذى صَنَعـا

ولو صَحَا القَلبُ عنها كان لى تَبَعَا	كَمْ من دَنِئٍ لهـا قـد كنتُ أَتَبَعُـهُ
أحبّ شيءٍ إلى الإنسان مـا مُنِعـا	وزادنى كلفًا فى الـحبّ أَن مُنِعَـت
مِنى التحيّةُ إن الموت قد نَزَعـا	اقْرَ السلاَم على لَيْلَى وَحقَّ لهـا
قَلَّ العَزاءُ وأبدَى القلبُ مـا جَزِعـا	أماتَ أم هو حَىٌّ فى البـلاد ؟ فقـد

His family reproached him of loving Leyla. He then recited this poem to them. According to the tradition, it is indicated as the one that gave him the name Majnūn "the Madman".

Contemplate, O poor madman, this heart snatched away

by an impossible love, which you never can appease.

The love and longing that I have for her

have a hold on my heart and dwell within it.

Blessed is the man in this earth who shares your life!

God has spared him from torments and worries,

while for me, before each of the letters that you have sent me,

can only burst into tears at each of their words.

I encourage my heart to flee her, it accepts. But as soon that I say

"It is best so", my longing for her only increases.

I cannot stop myself from loving this woman

and the love in my heart can only intensify its torments.

Many times I could have followed those you despise,

but my heart intoxicated by you would not have obeyed.

Passion intensifies the more it is curbed:

Man loves nothing more than the forbidden fruit!

May they send my greetings to Leyla,

it is necessary that they do it now. Death is on its way.

Am I dead or alive in this earth?

It is too unbearable for this impatient heart

which beats loud and cries![68]

(52)

خِيَامٌ بِنَجْدٍ دُونَهَا الطَّرْفُ يَقْصُرُ	أَحِنُّ إِلَى أَرْضِ الْحِجَازِ وَحَاجَتِى
أَجَلْ ، لاَ ، وَلكِنِّى عَلَى ذَاكَ أَنْظُرُ	وَمَا نَظَرِى مِنْ نَحْوِ نَجْدٍ بِنَافِعِى
لَعَيْنِكَ يَجْرِى مَاؤُهَا يَتَحَدَّرُ	أَفِى كُلِّ يَوْمٍ عَبْرَةٌ ثُمَّ نَظْرَةٌ
حَزِينٌ وَإِمَّا نَازِحٌ يَتَذَكَّرُ	مَتى يَسْتَرِيحُ القَلْبُ إِمَّا مُجَاوِرٌ
لَهَا الدَّهْرَ دَمْعٌ وَاكِفٌ يَتَحَدَّرُ	يَقُولُونَ كَمْ تَجْرِى مَدَامِعُ عَيْنِهِ
وَلْكِنَّهَا نَفْسٌ تَذُوبُ وَتَقْطُرُ	وَلَيسَ الَّذِى يَجْرِى مِنَ الْعَيْنِ مَاؤُهَا

I long for the earth of Al-Ḥidjāz,[69]

I need to see a camp in Najd.

But it is far away,

too far away,

it is invisible,

and it is of no use to look this way at Najd.

Is it good? Is it bad?

Continue! It is enough! It is too late.

I shall stay here and watch.

And in this manner! Day after day,

one look, one tear, one look.

Oh this water that fills my eyes and pours down!

When will peace come to my pounding heart?

It is either unhappy when she is near

or filled with longing when she is far.

They say: "See him crying.

She has destroyed him completely

and his tears keep on flowing."

But no, these are not tears

that are pouring down from my eyes,

but a soul that is gradually dripping.[70]

(53)

مُعَرَّقة تضْحَى إليه وتـخْصَرُ	سَلَبْتِ عظامى لحمَها فَتَرَكْتِهَا
قواريرُ فى أجوافها الريـح تَصْفِـر	وأخليتِها مـن مُخِّهـا وكأنهـا
علائقُها مما تخـاف وتحـذَرُ	إذا سمعت ذكر الحبيب تقطّـعت
بــى الضرُّ إلا أننــى أتَسَتَّـــرُ	خذى بيدى ثم انهضى بى تَبَيُّنِـى
علىَّ ولا لى عنكِ صَبْـرٌ فأصْبـرُ	فما حيلتى إن لـم تكن لكِ رحمـةٌ
رضاك ولكنـى مُـجِبٌ مُكفِّـر	فـواللهِ مـا قَصَّرْتُ فيمـا أظنُّـهُ
ولكنهـا نـفس تـذوب فتقطُـرُ	وليس الذى يجرى من العين ماؤهـا

My bones have not longer any skin,

you have undressed them

and left then naked in the sunlight

and in the cold night.

See, they are emptied from their marrow

and remind of some hollow reed pipes

through which the wind sighs.

One day you will hear it,

and then, terrified, you will remember

the one who loves you.

The fear in your confused soul

will break down all the inhibitions.

Take my hand, lift me up

and see carefully all that you have caused.

But no, I shall hide it. I am now destitute.

All of this is of no use if you do not feel any compassion,

and if I do not find enough strength to abandon you.

I have done everything in my power, O God,

to make her happy, and I am not anything else

but a loving man, who is unfaithful to You.

No, these are not tears, that are pouring down from my eyes,

but a soul that is gradually dripping![71]

(54)

إلى الـدار مـن مـاءِ الصبابـة أنظُرُ   نظرتُ كأنى مـن وراءِ زجاجـة

فأُغْشَى وطوراً تَـحْسِيَراِن فـأُبصِرُ   فعينـاىَ طـورًا تغَرَقـان مـن البُكَـا

ولكِنَّـه نَـفس تَـــذوب فتقطُـــرُ   وليس الذى يَهْمى من العين دمعُهـا

I looked at the camp

and I thought that I was seeing it behind a glass pane.

Love was rendering everything blurry,

and my eyes were drowning in tears

which were blinding me.

Other times, the water would withdraw,

and again I could see.

No, these are not tears

that are pouring down from my eyes,

but a soul that is gradually dripping![72]

(55)

وقفتُ لليلى بعد عشرين حِجَّـةً   بمنزلـةٍ فانهـلَّت العيـن تدمَـعُ

فأمـرض قلبـى حُبُّهـا وعذابهـا   وما للعِدَى من صبوةٍ كيف أصنعُ

وأتّبع ليلى حـيث سارتْ وودَّعت   ومـا النـاس إلا آلِـف ومُـوَدع

كـأن زمامًـا فـى الفـؤاد مُعلَّقًـا   تقود به حيث استَمرّت فأتبـعُ

أبـيت بَرْوْحـاتِ الطريـق كأننى   أخـو جِنَّـةٍ أوصالُـهُ تتقطَّـعُ

I shall not go farther away, O Leyla,

twenty years, this is a too long time.

I shall wait for you here,

crying over my misery.

My love for you

is my sick heart's slayer,

but against the enemy,

if this one is loved,

what can one do?

I go where Leyla goes

and then she leaves me.

This is life:

people reunite and separate.

I think I have put around my heart a leash:

Leyla drags me and after her I follow.

Darkness surrounds my path

and I am shaking,

as though I were mad

and my members were dislocating.[73]

(56)

عجبتُ لليلى كيف نامتْ وقد غفتْ   وليس لعينـى للمنـام سبيـل

ولمـا غفت عينى وما عـادة لهـا   بنـوم وقلبـى بالفـراق عليـل

أتانى خيـالٌ مـنك يـا ليـل زائـر   فكـادت له نـفسى الغـداةَ تـزولُ

خيـال لليلـى زارنـى بَعـد هَجْـرِه   ورام عتابِـى والعتـاب يطـولُ

———————

I am surprised that Leyla can fall asleep

when sleep cannot find its way any more to me.

When once, in spite of the separation's torments,

my eyes became heavy with sleep,

the beloved Leyla visited me.

- Oh she was so beautiful

that I almost died when I awoke! -

Leyla's spirit came to me

after having abandoned me

and silenced the complains

that have embittered me.[74]

(57)

ألا تـلك ليلى قـد ألَـمَّ لِمَامُهـا وكيف مع القوم الأعادى كلامُها

تمتَّـعْ بليلـى إنمـا أنت هامــة من الهـام يدنو كـل يـومٍ حِمَامُهـا

وبـاذر بليلى أُوْبـةَ الـركْب إنهـمْ متى يَرْجِعُوا يَحْرُمْ عليك لِمَامهـا

When Leyla's husband and her father had traveled one day to Mecca, she sent her maid to Majnūn to give him the message that he was invited to visit her one night. He stayed with her until the morning and she said to him before he left: "Come to me every night as long as the people are away," which he did. The last night, he recited these verses.

Leyla is now mine,

as I only can meet her sometimes.

I cannot visit Leyla

after that her people return.

I love Leyla!

Truly, she is the biggest passion

that Destiny threatens to take away from me

with every day that passes.

Alas! I must now be separated from Leyla!

The caravan has arrived.

I can never delight in Leyla's love

after that her people have returned.[75]

(58)

وَأَيَّامَ لاَ نَخْشَى على اللَّهْو نَاهِيَا	تَذكَّرْتُ لَيْلَى والسِّنِينَ الْخَوَالِيَا
بِلَيْلَى فَلَهَّانِى وما كُنْتُ لأَهِيَا	وَيَوْم كَظِلِّ الرُّمْحِ قَصَّرْتُ ظِلَّـهُ
بِذَاتِ الْغَضَى تُرجى الْمَطِىَّ النَّوَاجِيَا	بِثَمْدِينَ لاَحَتْ نَـارُ لَيْلَى وَصُحْبَتِـى
بَدَا فِى سَوَادِ اللَّيْـلِ فَـرْدًا يَمَانِيَـا	فَقَالَ بَصِيرُ الْقَوْمِ أَلْمَحْتُ كَوْكَبَا
بِعَلْيَا تَسَامَى ضَوْؤُهَا فَبَدَا لِيَـا	فَقُلْتُ لَهُ : بَلْ نَارُ لَيْلَى تَوَقَّدَتْ
وَلَيْتَ الْغَضَى مَاشَى الرَّكَابَ لَيَالِيَا	فَلَيْتَ رِكَابَ الْقَوْمِ لَمْ تَقْطَعِ الْغَضَى
إذا جِئْتُكُـمْ بِاللَّيْـلِ لَـمْ أَدْرِ مَاهِيَـا	فَيَا لَيْلَ كَمْ مِنْ حَاجَةٍ لِى مُهِمَّةٍ
خَلِيلاً إذَا أَنْزَفْتُ دَمْعِى، بَكَى لِيَا	خَلِيلَـىَّ إنْ تَبْكِيَانِـيَ أَلْتَـمِسْ
وَلاَ أُنْشِدُ الأَشْعَـارَ إلاَّ تَدَاوِيَـا	فَمَـا أُشْرِفُ الأَيْفَـاعَ إلاَّ صَبَابَـةً

I remember, O Leyla, the years that passed and all these days!

O continuous bliss, O light-heartedness!

O days you passed in a flash like the shadow of the lance,

and faster did your shadow disappear with Leyla!

You were happiness... I was not happy.

I remember! Thamdīn: we saw a fire glow, it was Leyla!

Our horses, urged by my companions,

galloped quickly towards al-Ghaḍā.

One of us with falcon sight said: "I see a star,

there alone, toward Yemen, in the heart of the night!".

And I said: "No, it is Leyla, this fire glowing high in the sky,

and it is for me that it has revealed itself."

Was it necessary, O my friends, to ride through al-Ghaḍā?

Why did we hurry there?

If only these places had taken us away with them in the night!

In me, O Leyla, so many desires and worries have multiplied.

If the night leads me to you, where are you?

The day that you tire of crying over me, O friends,

I shall find someone else who will cry.

His tears will pour when I shall be unable more to cry.

I have experienced passion already as a young man,

and if I am now writing poems it is only to calm my despair.

وَقَدْ يَجْمَعُ اللهُ الشَّتِيتَيْنِ بَعْدَمَا   يَظُنَّانِ كُـلَّ الظَّـنِّ أَنْ لاَ تَلاَقِـيَـا

لَحَى اللهُ أَقْوَامَـا يَقُولُـونَ إِنَّـا   وَجَدْنَا طَوَالَ الدَّهْرِ لِلْحُبِّ شَافِـيَا

وَعَهْدِى بِلَيْلَى وَهْىَ ذاتُ مُؤَصَّدٍ   تَـرُدُّ عَلَيْنَـا بِالْـعَشِيِّ المَوَاشِيَا

فَشَبَّ بَنُو لَيْلَى وَشَبَّ بَنُو ابْنِهَـا   وَأَعْلاَقُ لَيْلَى فِى فُؤَادِى كَمَا هِيَا

إِذَا مَا جَلَسْنَا مَجْـلِسًا نَسْتَلِـذُّهُ   تَـوَاشَوْا بَنَـا حَتَّـى أَمَـلَّ مَكَانَـا

سَقَى اللهُ جَارَاتٍ لِلَيْلَى تَبَاعَـدَتْ   بِهِنَّ النَّوَى حَيْثُ اخْتَلَلْنَ المطَالِبَا

وَلَمْ يُنْسِنِى لَيْلَى افْتِقَـارٌ وَلاَ غِنًى   وَلاَ تَوْبَةٌ حَتَّى احْتَضَنْتُ السَّوَارِيَا

وَلاَ نِسْوَةٌ صُبِّغْـنَ كَبْـدَاءَ جَلْعَـدَا   لِتُشْبِهَ لَيْلَى ثُـمَّ عَرَضْتَهَا لِيَـا

خَلِيلَـيَّ لاَ وَاللهِ لاَ أَمْـلِكُ الَّـذِى   قَضَى اللهُ فِى لَيْلَى وَلاَ مَا قضَى لِيا

قضَاهَا لِغَيْـرِى وَابْتَلاَنِـى بِحُبِّهـا   فَهَـلاَّ بِشَىءٍ غَيْـرِ لَيْلَى ابْتَلاَنِيَـا

Sometimes God unites the tormented lovers
who never believed more that they would unite.
Damn them, O God, all those who say:
"Life has done its work and cured your love.
They are long time ago these days when Leyla, clothed in linen,
brought back the cattle home in the evenings!"
But her children and children's children can grow up
everything that is hers has a place like her in my heart.
If we sat alone in a beautiful secluded place to talk,
we became exposed. These places now horrify me!
May God shower Leyla and her girlfriends with His good deeds
when they pitch their camps in remote valleys!
Whether I am rich or poor I can never forget her,
and when at night, a long road takes me
to my lover's arms I do not regret anything!
O women, it is of no use to put on make-up
on someone among you who is beautiful
with nice curves, and then show her to me and say:
"This is Leyla!"
Alas my friends! I must endure, poor me,
the destiny that has fallen upon us both.
God gives her to another man and breaks my heart:
could he not have destroyed me in another way?

وَخَبَّرْتُمَانِـــى أَنَّ تَيْمَـــاءَ مَنْـــزِلٌ   لِلَيْلَى إِذَا مَا الصَّيْفُ أَلْقَى المَرَاسِيَا

فَهٰذِى شُهُورُ الصَّيْفِ عَنَّا قَدِ انْقضتْ   فَمَا لِلنَّوَى تَرْمِى بِلَيْلَى المَرَامِيَا

فَلَـــوْ أَنَّ وَاشٍ بِالْيَمَامَـــةِ دَارُهُ   وَدَارِى بِأُعْلَى حَضْرَ مَوْتَ آهْتَدَى لِيا

وَمَـاذَا لَهُـمْ لاَ أَحْسَنَ اللهُ حَالَهُـمْ   مِنَ الحَظِّ فِى تصْرِيمِ لَيْلَى حَبَالِيا

وَقَدْ كُنْتُ أَعْلُو حُبَّ لَيْلَى فَلَمْ يَـزَلْ   بِىَ النَّقْضُ وَالْإِبْرَامُ حَتَّى عَلاَنِيَا

فَيَا رَبِّ سَوِّ الـحُبَّ بَيْنِى وَبَيْنَهَا   يَكُـونُ كَفَافًا لاَ عَلَـىَّ وَلاَ لِيَـا

فَمَا طلَعَ النَّجْمُ الَّذِى يُهْتَدَى بِـهِ   وَلاَ الصُّبْحُ إِلاَّ هيَّجَا ذِكْرَهـا لِيَـا

وَلاَ سِرْتُ مِيلاً مِنْ دِمَشْقَ وَلاَ بَـدَا   سُهَيْـلٌ لِأَهْـلِ الشَّامِ إِلاَّ بَـدا لِيَـا

You have said: "Leyla has pitched her tent in Taymāʾ.[76]

All of the summer she will be there."

But I have seen the months of the summer flee.

Oh! Why is there such a long road, O Leyla,

that carries you away and separates you from me?

Suppose that I live up there, [77] in Ḥaḍramawt,[78]

and then a slanderer comes to Yamāma,

he will surely find his way to me!

But why do they all rejoice,

Oh! May God damn them, to know

that the ties between Leyla and me are now broken?

- I who have always wanted to control this love,

that at the end, when so much was taken away from me,

I found my master. -

Oh! May the love between her and me become mutual,

may it remain strong and never cause my defeat or success!

May the star rise

and show me the way,

may the morning come a

nd awake my longing.

A whole mile can separate me from Damascus:

if Canopus[79] appears to Damascus's people,

it is she whom I see.

وَلاَ سُمِّيَتْ عِنْدِى لَهَا مِنْ سَمِيَّةٍ — مِنَ النَّاسِ إِلاَّ بَلَّ دَمْعِى رِدَائِيَا

وَلاَ هَمَّتِ الرِّيحُ الجَنُوبُ لِأَرْضِهَا — مِنَ اللَّيْلِ إِلاَّ بِتُّ لِلرِّيحِ حَانِيَا

فَإِنْ تَمْنَعُوا لَيْلَى وَتَحْمُوا بِلاَدَهَا — عَلَىَّ فَلَنْ تَحْمُوا عَلَىَّ الْقَوَافِيَا

فَأَشْهَدُ عِنْدَ اللهِ أَنِّى أُحِبُّهَا — فَهٰذَا لَهَا عِنْدِى فَمَا عِنْدَهَا لِيَا

قَضَى اللهُ بِالْمَعْرُوفِ مِنْهَا لِغَيْرِنَا — وَبِالشَّوْقِ مِنِّى وَالْغَرَام قَضَى لِيَا

وَإِنَّ الَّذِى أَمَّلْتُ يَا أُمَّ مَالِكِ — أَشَابَ فُوَيْدِى وَاسْتَهَامَ فُؤَادِيَا

أَعُدُّ اللَّيَالِى لَيْلَةً بَعْدَ لَيْلَةٍ — وَقَدْ عِشْتُ دَهْرًا لاَ أَعُدُّ اللَّيَالِيَا

وَأَخْرُجُ مِنْ بَيْنِ الْبُيُوتِ لَعَلَّنِى — أُحَدِّثُ عَنْكِ النَّفْسَ بِاللَّيْلِ خَالِيَا

أَرَانِى إِذَا صَلَّيْتُ يَمَّمْتُ نَحْوَهَا — بِوَجْهِى وَإِنْ كَانَ الْمُصَلَّى وَرَائِيَا

وَمَا بِىَ إِشْرَاكٌ وَلٰكِنَّ حُبَّهَا — وَعُظْمَ الجَوَى أَعْيَا الطَّبِيبَ الْمُدَاوِيَا

أُحِبُّ مِنَ الْأَسْمَاءِ مَا وَافَقَ اسْمَهَا — أَوْ أَشْبَهَهُ أَوْ كَانَ مِنْهُ مُدَانِيَا

When one talks in my presence of another Leyla,

the tears immediately start to wet my garments;

and if the southern wind blows toward her country,

I find myself in the night falling in love with the wind!

Are they forbidding me to meet Leyla?

Are they watching over her dwelling?

They cannot take away the verses from me!

I admit before God that I love you, O Leyla:

You rule my heart, but what am I to you?

God chooses: he smiles to another and gives you to him.

God decides: he gives me love's longing and despair.

I have dreamt too long of happy days, O Umm Mālik:

my hair has become grey and my reason has weakened.

Night after night, and I am counting the nights,

- I who have lived a life before, without counting them! -

I leave the camp here, I have the ability,

when I am alone in the night and thinking of you to see you!

You draw my looks to you even during the prayer,

but I must learn to look forward and not backward![80]

I am not an unbeliever, but my passion for you

awakes my sorrow and renders a doctor helpless.

A name, for me, is loveable

if it goes well with yours or resembles it.

خَلِيلَيَّ لَيْلَى أَكْبَرُ الْحَاجِ وَالْمُنَى ... فَمَنْ لِى بِلَيْلَى أَوْ فَمَنْ ذا لَها بِيَا

لَعَمْرِى لقد أَبْكَيْتِنِى يَا حَمَامَةَ الْعَقِيـ ... ـقِ وَأَبْكَيْتِ الْعُيُـونَ الْبَوَاكِيَـا

خَلِيلَيَّ مَا أَرْجُو مِنَ الْعَيْشِ بَعْدَمَا ... أَرَى حَاجَتِى تُشْرَى وَلاَ تُشْتَرَى لِيَا

وَنُجْـرِمُ لَيْلَى ثُـمَّ تَزْعُـمُ أَنِّـى ... سَلَوْتُ وَلاَ يَخْفَى عَلى النَّاسِ مَا بِيَا

فَلَـمْ أَرَ مِثْلَيْنَـا خَلِيلَـىْ صَبَابَــةٍ ... أَشدَّ عَلَى رَغْمِ الْأَعَـادِى تصَافِيَـا

خَلِيلاَنِ لاَ نَرْجُو اللِّقَاءَ وَلاَ نَـرَى ... خَلِيلَيْـنِ إلاَّ يَرْجُـوَان تلاَقِيَـا

وَإنِّى لَأَسْتَحْيِيكِ أَنْ تَعْرِضَ الْمُنَى ... بِوَصْلِكِ أَوْ أَنْ تَعْرِضِى فى الْمُنَى لِيَا

She is my most beautiful dream, O friends,

or the longing that destroys!

The one who sides with me sides with her,

the one who sides with her sides with me.

O al-ᶜAqīq's[81] pigeon, how many tears do I owe you!

You know it well, these eyes are only crying for you.

What can I expect from life, my friends,

when I see my happiness put up for auction

and being bought by someone else?

Leyla treats me badly, and then she says:

"He is forgetting me."

But everyone knows in which state I am!

Among friends and lovers,

we are the ideal couple:

one soul in two bodies,

in spite of all our enemies.

We are two friends with no hope of reuniting;

the only ones in the world?

No. But let them show us two friends who decline from uniting!

It is true that I fear you,

I fear of seeing you again,

I fear even that life fulfills this desire.

I fear almost to see you in my dreams!

يَقُولُ أُنَاسٌ عَلَّ مَجْنُونَ عَامِرٍ   يَرُومُ سُلُوًّا قُلْتُ أَنَّى لِمَا بِيَا

بِىَ الْيَأْسُ أَوْ دَاءُ الهُيَامِ أَصَابَنِى   فَإِيَّاكَ عَنِّى لاَ يَكُنْ بِكِ مَا بِيَا

إِذَا مَا اسْتَطَالَ الدَّهْرُ يَا أُمَّ مَالِكٍ   فَشَأْنُ المَنَايَا الْقَاضِيَاتِ وَشَانِيَا

إِذَا اكْتُحَلَتْ عَيْنِى بِعَيْنِكِ لَمْ تَزَلْ   بِخَيْرٍ وَجَلَّتْ غَمْرَةً عَنْ فُؤَادِيَا

فَأَنْتِ الَّتِى إِنْ شِئْتِ أَشْقَيْتِ عِيشَتِى   وَأَنْتِ الَّتِى إِنْ شِئْتِ أَنْعَمْتِ بَالِيَا

وَأَنْتِ الَّتِى مَا مِنْ صَدِيقٍ وَلاَ عِدًا   يَرَى نِضْوَ مَا أَبْقَيْتِ إِلاَّ رَثَى لِيَا

أَمَضْرُوبَةٌ لَيْلَى عَلَى أَنْ أَزُورَهَا   وَمُتَّخَذٌ ذَنْبًا لَهَا أَنْ تَرَانِيَا

I hear them saying: "Majnūn from the tribe of ᶜĀmir

needs only to take a rest."

And I answer: "How can I do that?

I am suffering, I am mad of passion,

I am desperate.

Do not come close to me

so that you will not be contaminated!"

O Umm Mālik, the time will pass like that,

and then the fatal moment will arrive.

Destiny will carry my name:

everything will be said.

O the happiness of my eyes

when they lose themselves in your eyes,

ruled by a burning heart,

drowning in tears and clear!

It is you who decide if you want to make my life a hell,

it is you who decide if you want to make me happy.

Because of you, I am now a poor shadow of myself,

cried over by all, regardless of whether they hate or love me.

Shall they hit and punish Leyla

every time that I visit her,

and when she sees me, be angry at her

and even accuse her of committing a sin?

أُصَانِعُ رَحْلِى أَنْ يَمِيلَ حِيَالِيَا	إِذَا سِرْتُ فِى الْأَرْضِ الْفَضَاءِ رَأَيْتُنِى
شِمَالًا يُنَازِعْنِى الْهَوَى عَنْ شِمَالِيَا	يَمِينًا إِذَا كَانَتْ يَمِينًا وَإِنْ تَكُنْ
لَعَلَّ خَيَالًا مِنْكِ يَلْقَى خَيَالِيَا	وَإِنِّى لَأَسْتَغْشِى وَمَا بِىَ نَعْسَةٌ
وَأَنَّى لَا أُلْفِى لَهَا الدَّهْرَ رَاقِيَا	هِىَ السِّحْرُ إِلَّا أَنَّ لِلسِّحْرِ رُقْيَةً
كَفَا لِمَطَايَانَا بِذِكْرَاكِ هَادِيَا	إِذَا نَحْنُ أَدْلَجْنَا وَأَنْتِ أَمَامَنَا
لَها وَهَجٌ مُسْتَضْرَمٌ فِى فُؤَادِيَا	ذَكَتْ نَارُ شَوْقِى فِى فُؤَادِى فَأَصْبَحْتُ
عَلَيْنَا فَقَدْ أَمْسَى هَوَانَا يَمَانِيَا	أَلَا أَيُّها الرَّكْبُ الْيَمَانُونَ عَرِّجُوا

Every time that I start a journey on this earth,

I caress my camel mare

and lead her to where my heart inclines.

Toward the East and South if Leyla calls me,

but even stronger, if Leyla waits for me,

is the longing to the North

that almost pulls me out of the saddle!

I want, I want to sleep,

but sleep refuses to come to me:

perhaps that your ghost will soon appear?

She is a sorceress; Alas! But even witchcraft

can sometimes be defeated by other powers

unless when it concerns me,

whom Leyla always holds in her spell.

When we are getting nearer to you

as the night surprises us,

our mounts are only led by my thoughts of you.

Ruled by the flames of desire

my heart releases the rein.

O consuming glow,

O burning heart!

Take a rest by us, O Yemenite riders,

for our love is passing the night in Yemen.

أَسَائِلُكُمْ هَـلْ سَالَ نُعْمَـانُ بَعْدَنَـا ∗ وَحُبَّ إِلَيْنَا بَطـنُ نُعْمَـانَ وَادِيَـا

أَلاَ يَا حَمَامَىْ بَطْنِ نُعْمَانَ هِجْتُمَـا ∗ عَلَـى الهَـوَى لَمَّـا تَغَنَّيْتُمَـا لِيَـا

وَأَبْكَيْتُمَانِى وَسْطَ صَحْبِى وَلَمْ أَكُنْ ∗ أُبَالِى دُمُوعَ الْعَيْنِ لَوْ كُنْتُ خَالِيَـا

وَيَـا أَيُّهَـا الْقُمْرِيَّـانِ تَجَاوَبَـا ∗ بِلَحْنَيْكُمَـا ثُـمَّ اسْجَعَـا عَلَّلاَنِيَـا

فَـإِنْ أَنْتُمَـا اسْتَطْرَبْتُمَا أَوْ أَرَدْتُمَـا ∗ لَحَاقًـا بِأَطْـلاَلِ الْـغَضَى فَاتْبَعَانِيَـا

أَلاَ لَيْتَ شِعْرِى مَا لِلَيْلَى وَمَالِيَـا ∗ وَمَا لِلصِّبَا مِنْ بَعْدِ شَيْبٍ عَلاَنِيَـا

أَلاَ أَيُّهَـا الْـوَاشِى بِلَيْلَـى أَلاَ تَـرَى ∗ إِلَى مَنْ تَشِيهَا أَوْ بِمَنْ جِئْتُ وَاشِيَـا

لَئِنْ ظَعَنَ الْأَحْبَابُ يَا أُمَّ مَالِكِ ∗ فَمَا ظَعَنَ الْـحُبُّ الَّـذِى فِى فُؤَادِيَـا

Tell me when we have gone away,

did the creek of Naᶜmān continue to flow,

and did the valley continue to lead forth its streams to us

like in an act of love?

O Naᶜmān's pigeons, what a storm in my heart

you have awaken when you sang for me!

When one is alone, one's tears do not harm one's honor,

but see, I have cried in front of my followers.

O pigeons, sing, exchange your answers,

coo melodies, rock my despair,

and may your songs predict a happy meeting

in the camp of al-Ghaḍā.

Follow me!

How shall I know, O Leyla,

if I ever will know it one day,

among all these white hairs that cover my head,

which are my part, your part or love's part?

The slanderers are saying evil things about you,

but do they know to whom

and about whom they are talking like this?

'They say that the lovers,

O Umm Mālik, disappear,

but the passion in my heart for ever glows.

فَيَا رَبِّ إِذْ صَيَّرْتَ لَيْلَى هِيَ الْمُنَى   فَزِنِّى بِعَيْنَيْهَا كَمَا زِنْتَهَا لِيَا

وَإِلاَّ فَبَغِّضْهَا إِلَــيَّ وَأَهْلَهَـــا   فَإِنِّى بِلَيْلَى قَـدْ لَقِـيتُ الدَّوَاهِيَـا

عَلَى مِثْـل لَيْلَى يَقْتُـلُ المَرْءُ نَفْسَهُ   وَإِنْ كُنْتُ مِنْ لَيْلَى عَلَى الْيَأْسِ طَاوِيَا

خَلِيلَـيَّ إِنَّ ضَنُّــوا بِلَيْلَـى فقرِّبَـــا   لِىَ النَّعْشَ وَالْأَكْفانَ وَاسْتغْفِرَا لِيَا

I beg of you, my God,

if you have made Leyla to be my destiny,

then make her see me with the same loving eyes

that I am seeing her with!

Or else, free me from this passion,

as meeting her has been meeting my misfortune.

Oh! For a woman like Leyla

any man would want to kill himself,

even if like me, he can accustom himself to despair.

If they forbid me to meet her,

then you could, O my friends,

prepare for me the bed of death and the shroud,

and pray to God that He has Mercy on me![82]

(59)

أَرِقْتُ وَعادَنـى هَـمٌّ جَديــدُ   فَجِسْمِى لِلْهَـوَى نِضْوٌ بَلِيـدُ

أُراعِـى الْفَرْقَدَيْـنِ مـع الثُّرَيَّـا   كذاك الْـحُبُّ أَهْوَنُـهُ شَدِيـدُ

عَلِـقْتُ مَلِيحَـةَ الْخَدَّيْـنِ وَرْدًا   تُشابه حُسْنَ مَطْلَعِهَا السُّعُودُ

أَهِيــمُ بِذِكرِهَـا وَأَظَـلُّ صَبًّــا   وَعَيْنِى بِالدُّمُوعِ لها تجُـودُ

أَلاَ يا لَيْتَ لَحْدَكِ كان لَحْـدِى   إذا ضَمَّتْ جَنَائِزَنَا اللحـودُ

Sleep left me

and opened the way for new torments,

and love weakened my body's movements.

I looked at the Little Bear and the Pleiades.

Love is like this,

the smallest things become a burden through it.

This beautiful woman with the rosy cheeks

whom I have fallen in love with,

I see her in front of me,

a glowing and clear star,

rising in the sky.

I love you,

I am madly in love with you,

I am thinking of you only.

It is for you that my eyes are crying rivers.

I would have wanted,

I would have wanted

that your death were my death,

and that one only grave

held both our bodies![83]

(60)

أَيَا قَبْرَ لَيْلَى لـو شَهِدْنَاك أُعْـوَلَتْ   عَلَيْكَ نِسَاءٌ مِنْ فَصِيحٍ ومِنْ عَجَمْ

ويـا قبـرَ ليلى أُكْرِمَــنَّ مَحَلَّهَــا   يَكُنْ لك مـا عِشْنَا عَلَيْنَا بها نِعَمْ

ويـا قبـرَ ليلى إن لَيْلَــى غريبَـــة   بأُرْضِكَ لا خالٌ لَدَيْها ولا ابْنُ عَمْ

ويا قبرَ ليلى مـا تَضَمَّـنْتَ قَبْلهَـا   شَبِيهًا لِلَيْلَى ذا عَفَافٍ وذا كَـرمْ

ويـا قبرَ ليلى غـابَتِ الْيَـوْمَ أُمُّهـا   وَخَالَتُهَـا وَالْحَافِظُـونَ لهـا الذِّمَـمْ

O Leyla's grave,

if the women of Arabia and Persia saw you now

they would yell out mourning screams!

O Leyla's grave,

protect always in honor

the one who brought grace into our life!

O Leyla's grave,

she is now a stranger,

there is no uncle or cousin

who is standing by her side!

Never before, O grave,

you have embraced

such a noble and pure woman as Leyla!

O Leyla's grave,

they are far away today,

her mother, her aunt

and all those who have protected her life![84]

(61)

هل فُرِّجَتْ عنكمُ مُذْ مِتُّمُ الكُـرَبُ	لو سِيلَ أَهْلُ الْهَوَى من بعد مَوْتِهِـمُ
لكنَّ نار الهوى فى القـلب تَلْتَـهبُ	لقال صادِقُهُـمْ أنْ قـد بَلِـى جَسَدِى
وإنَّ بالدمع عَيْنَ الرُّوح تَـنْسَكِبُ	جفَّتْ مَدامعُ عَيْنِ الْجِسْم حينَ بَكى

———————————

If beyond death

one asked the lovers:

"O lovers, have you become relieved

of your torments?"

They will answer honestly:

"It is true that our bodies

have turned into ashes,

but the fire of love

still burns in our hearts.

Our body's eyes,

when they want to express our sorrow,

have tears that have dried up in their corners,

but our soul's eyes, they,

have tears that incessantly flow!"[85]

(62)

رِيَاضًا مِنَ الْحَوْذَانِ فِى بَلَدٍ قَفْرِ	أَلاَ لَيْتَنَا كُنَّا غَزَالَيْنِ نَرْتَعِى
نَطِيرُ وَنَأْوِى بِالْعَشِيِّ إِلَى وَكْرِ	أَلا لَيتَنَا كُنَّا حَمَامَىْ مَفَـازَةٍ
إِذَا نَحْنُ أَمْسَيْنَا نُلَجِّجُ فِى الْبَحْرِ	أَلا لَيتَنَا حُوتَانِ فِى الْبَحْرِ نَرْئِمِى
نَصِيرُ إِذَا مِتْنَا ضَجِيعَيْنِ فِى قَبْرِ	وَيَا لَيتَنَا نَحْيَا جَمِيعًا وَلَيتَنَـا
وَنُقْرَن يوم الْبَعْثِ وَالْحَشْرِ وَالنَّشْرِ	ضَجِيعَيْنِ فِى قَبْرٍ عَنِ النَّاسِ مُعْزَلِ

I wish we were

two deer grazing in distant valleys,

in green fields where the _Ḥawzān_-herbs[86] grow.

I wish we were two doves in the desert,

flying to our nest in the evening.

I wish we were two sharks in the streams,

rocked in the evening by the big sea.

I dream, I see us:

my life, your life, together!

I see, I dream, and even death unites us,

in the grave's bed, side by side, together!

A resting place far away from the world,

O well-concealed grave!

There we will rise

to experience the resurrection's day,

the new life and the eternal union![87]

Notes to the Poems

[1] Metre *wāfir*. The rhyme is *-āʾu*. See *Dīwān* nr. 2 and *Zahra* 329.

[2] Al-Batīl is a mountain in Najd.

[3] Metre *ṭawīl*. The rhyme is *-aṣdi*. See *Dīwān* nr. 94, *Basṭ* 75, *Aghānī* II, 23 and *Maṣāriʿ* 271.

[4] Metre *ṭawīl*. The rhyme is *-mu (-amu* or *-umu)*. See *Dīwān* nr. 238 and *Basṭ* 94.

[5] Metre *ṭawīl*. The rhyme is *-ādiyā*. See *Dīwān* nr. 315.

[6] Metre *ṭawīl*. The rhyme is *-iyā*. See ibid nr. 314 and *Zahra* 349.

[7] The rhyme is *-aʿu*. See *Dīwān* nr. 176.

[8] Metre *ṭawīl*. The rhyme is *-tu (-ītu* or *-ūtu)*. See ibid nr. 58, *Basṭ* 80 and *Zahra* 208.

[9] The rhyme is -*§mi*. See *Dīwān* nr. 258 and *Basṭ* 93.

[10] The rhyme is -*aqu*. See *Dīwān* nr. 197 and *Basṭ* 80.

[11] Metre *ṭawīl*. The rhyme is -*ūdihā*. See *Dīwān* nr. 88 and *Basṭ* 89.

[12] The rhyme is -*li*. See *Dīwān* nr. 224.

[13] The rhyme is -*ri*. See ibid nr. 149.

[14] Metre *ṭawīl*. The rhyme is -*a§ri*. See ibid nr. 143.

[15] Metre *ṭawīl*. The rhyme is -*&bi*. See ibid nr. 47.

[16] Metre *ṭawīl*. The rhyme is -*āni*. See ibid nr. 283.

[17] Metre *ṭawīl*. The rhyme is -*āʾibu*. See ibid nr. 5 and *Basṭ* 89.

[18] Metre *wāfir*. The rhyme is -*ārā*. See *Dīwān* nr. 155.

The house symbolizes the tent and the walls the tent's gore

[19] Metre *wāfir*. The rhyme is -*ābā*. See ibid nr. 54.

[20] Metre *ṭawīl*. The rhyme is -*ībuhā*. See ibid nr. 40 and *Basṭ* 94.

[21] See *Dīwān* nr. 41.

[22] See ibid nr. 239. The rhyme is -*amu*.

[23] Metre *ṭawīl*. The rhyme is -*ībuhā*. See ibid nr. 38, *Basṭ* 93 and *Zahra* 120.

[24] Metre *ṭawīl*. The rhyme is -*buhā (-ibuhā* or -*ubuhā*. See *Dīwān* nr. 39 and *Zahra* 120.

The last verses are understood as though Majnūn has identified himself with the wolf and does not want to live any more if he cannot continue to wander around the camp.

[25] Metre *ṭawīl*. The rhyme is -*buhā* (-*ībuhā* or -*ūbuhā*). See *Dīwān* nr. 37 and *Masālik* IX, 140.

[26] Metre *ṭawīl*. The rhyme is -*qu* (-*īqu* or -*ūqu*). See *Dīwān* nr. 199, *Tazyīn* 62 and *Amālī* I, 197.

[27] Metre *ṭawīl*. The rhyme is -*§du*. See *Dīwān* nr. 74, *Aghānī* II, 65, and *Zahra* 220.

[28] Al-ᶜĀmirīya indicates that Leyla pertains to the Banū ᶜĀmir tribe.

[29] Metre *wāfir*. The rhyme is -*āḥu*. See *Dīwān* nr. 64, *Basṭ* 89, *Aghānī* II, 48, 62, 89, 92 and *Zahra* 159-160.

[30] One can compare the theme of the kiss with the one in Baudelaire's poem *Le Vampire* in *Les Fleurs du Mal:*

"Tes baisers ressusciteraient
Le cadavre de ton vampire."
(*"Your kiss would soon resuscitate
The cold cadaver of your vampire."*) See *The Flowers of Evil.*

[31] Metre *ṭawīl*. The rhyme is -*ītu*. See *Dīwān* nr. 59.

[32] Metre *ṭawīl*. The rhyme is *ā§idi*. See ibid nr. 90 and *Zahra* 439.

[33] The word that the poet uses to refer to the earth's heightening is *mankib* "shoulder", which is a metaphor for "hill".

[34] The poet refers to *ṣadā*, which according to the pre-Islamic beliefs refers to an invisible bird that holds the dead person's soul and flies over his/her grave, cf. *Arabic-English Lexicon* II, 1670-1671.

[35] I am reminded of the verses written by the Swedish poet Esaias Tegnér (1782-1846) in his poem "Den döde" *(The Dead one")*, see *Dikt* p. 284:

"ty döden själv kan ej min kärlek hämma
och var jag är förnimmer jag din stämma"
(*"As death itself cannot curb my love,
And wherever I am I can hear your voice"*).

[36] Metre *ṭawīl*. The rhyme is *-bu (-abu, -ibu* or *-ubu)*. See *Dīwān* nr. 7, *Aghānī* II, 55 and *Zahra* 333.

[37] Metre *ṭawīl*. The rhyme is *-muhā*. See *Dīwān* nr. 254.

[38] Thabīr is a famous mountain in Mekka.

[39] Metre *ṭawīl*. The rhyme is *-bu (-abu* or *-ibu)*. See *Dīwān* nr. 8, *Aghānī* II, 55 and *Zahra* 333.

[40] "The damned", literally *ahl al-nār* "the people of hell".

[41] Metre *wāfir*. The rhyme is *-ūdu*. See *Dīwān* nr. 83.

[42] Metre *ṭawīl*. The rhyme is *-iruh*. See ibid nr. 127.

[43] Metre *ṭawīl*. The rhyme is *-ābi*. See ibid nr. 43 and *Basṭ* 90.

[44] The tradition describes Majnūn "the madman" as playing with stones and drawing in the sand.

[45] Metre *ṭawīl*. The rhyme is *-u (-aʾu* or *-uʾu)*. See *Dīwān* nr. 173 and *Basṭ* 89.

⁴⁶ Metre *ṭawīl*. The rhyme is *-ūᶜuhā*. See *Dīwān* nr. 183 and *Basṭ* 91.

⁴⁷ Metre *ṭawīl*. The rhyme is *-šlu*. See *Dīwān* nr. 208, *Aghānī* II, 46, *Tazyīn* 54 and *Basṭ* 72, 73.

⁴⁸ The amulet hangs around the child's neck in order to protect him/her against the evil eye.

⁴⁹ Metre *ṭawīl*. The rhyme is *-mah (-āšimuh* or *āšumuh)*. See *Dīwān* nr. 247, *Basṭ* 83 and *Aghānī* II, 6.

⁵⁰ The crow symbolizes the lovers' separation.

⁵¹ Metre *ṭawīl*. The rhyme is *-īru*. See *Dīwān* nr. 124, *Basṭ* 84, *Amālī* I, 183, *Samt* 451 and *Zahra* 249.

⁵² Metre *ṭawīl*. The rhyme is *-āluhā*. See *Dīwān* nr. 220, *Basṭ* 75, *Tazyīn* 66 and *Maṣāriᶜ* 270.

⁵³ Minā is one of Mecca's pilgrim places.

⁵⁴ Al-Khayf is the name of a mosque in Minā.

⁵⁵ Metre *ṭawīl*. The rhyme is *-šri*. See *Dīwān* nr. 144, *Basṭ* 75, 85, *Zahra* 167-168 and *Masālik* IX, 142.

⁵⁶ Metre *ṭawīl*. The rhyme is *-ašli*. See *Dīwān* nr. 227.

⁵⁷ Metre *wāfir*. The rhyme is *-bu (ibu* or *-ubu)*. See ibid nr. 30.

⁵⁸ *Ḥaythu asta'mana l-waḥshu* "[in this place] where the beasts are safe," refers to the prohibition of killing animals in and around Kaᶜba in Mecca.

⁵⁹ Al-Ḥaṭīm is a place in Mekka.

⁶⁰ Metre *ṭawīl*. The rhyme is *-buhā (-ībuhā* or *-ūbuhā)*. See *Dīwān* nr. 33, *Basṭ* 75, 92, *Samt* 900 and *Maṣāriᶜ* 251.

[61] Na‑cmān is a region that Leyla usually visits.

[62] Metre *ṭawīl*. The rhyme is -*muhā* (-*īmuhā* or -*ūmuhā*). See *Dīwān* nr. 251, *Aghānī* II, 26, *Tazyīn* 60 and *Zahra* 221, 231.

[63] Metre *ṭawīl*. The rhyme is -*abu*. See *Dīwān* nr. 6, *Basṭ* 89 and *Masālik* IX, 143.

[64] Metre *basīṭ*. The rhyme is -*bu* (-*abu*, -*ibu* or -*ubu*). See *Dīwān* nr. 11.

[65] Metre *ṭawīl*. The rhyme is -*buhā* (-*ībuhā* or -*ūbuhā*). See ibid nr. 34 and *Masālik* IX, 140.

[66] Jilhatān is a place which is hard to identify, cf. *Ṣifat jazīrat al-ᶜarab* 220.

[67] Metre *ṭawīl*. The rhyme is -*mu* (-*īmu* or -*ūmu*). See *Dīwān* nr. 246, *Aghānī* II, 59 and *Zahra* 42.

[68] Metre *basīṭ*. The rhyme is -*ᶜā*. See *Dīwān* nr. 191 and *Aghānī* II, 37.

[69] Al-Ḥidjāz is a mountainous province in the Arabian Peninsula that runs along the west-central coast. Najd is a region in central Saudi Arabia, comprising a rocky plateau sloping eastward from al-Ḥidjāz.

[70] Metre *ṭawīl*. The rhyme is -*ru* (-*aru*, -*iru* or -*uru*). See *Dīwān* nr. 116 and *Zahra* 203.

[71] Metre *ṭawīl*. The rhyme is -*ru* (-*aru*, -*iru* or –*uru*). See *Dīwān* nr. 117, *Tārīkh Baghdād* X, 211, *Tazyīn* 64 and *Amālī* I, 162.

[72] Metre *ṭawīl*. The rhyme is -*ru* (-*iru* or -*uru*). See *Dīwān* nr. 118, *Zahra* 295, *Amālī* I, 208 and *Aghānī* XVII, 138.

[73] Metre *ṭawīl*. The rhyme is *ᶜu*. See *Dīwān* nr. 172.

[74] The rhyme is *-lu*. See ibid nr. 215.

[75] The rhyme is *–uhā*. See ibid nr. 249 and *Aghānī* II, 72.

[76] Taymāʾ is an oasis in North Arabia.

[77] Up there refers to the mountains of the country.

[78] Ḥaḍramawt is a province in South Arabia. These verses have been mentioned and translated in my book *Arabic Morphology* 102-103.

[79] "Canopus" *suhayl* shows the direction to the beloved or symbolizes her.

[80] Forward and not backward: it is understood here that Leyla is standing among the women behind the men during the prayer and that Majnūn is looking backward at her instead of looking forward as the others in the direction of Mecca.

[81] Al-ᶜAqīq refers to a valley.

[82] Metre *ṭawīl*. The rhyme is *-āṣiyā*. See *Dīwān* nr. 307, *Basṭ* 85-89, *Masālik* IX, 138, 143, 144, *Aghānī* I, 8, 417, II, 10, 34, 36, 40, 54, 68, 69, 70, 77, 78, 93, IV, 291, 292, *Zahra* 26, 28, 40, 260, 303, 332, *Maṣāriᶜ* 238, *Amālī* I, 215, 221 and *Khizāna* IV, 295.

This poem is called *al-muʾnisa* "the reliable one" and is the longest in the collection.

[83] Metre *wāfir*. The rhyme is *-&du (-īdu* or *-ūdu)*. See *Dīwān* nr. 81.

[84] Metre *ṭawīl*. The rhyme is *-am*. See ibid nr. 257 and *Maṣāriᶜ* 296-297.

[85] Metre *basīṭ*. The rhyme is *-bu (-abu* or *-ibu)*. See *Dīwān* nr. 12.

[86] *Ḥawzān* is a herb that grows in the plains and that tastes good.

[87] Metre *ṭawīl*. The rhyme is *-a&ri*. See *ibid* nr. 145.

Bibliography

Arabic-English Lexicon = *Arabic-English Lexicon*, Lane, 2 Band, Cambridge 1984.

Aghānī = *Al-Aghānī*, Maṭbaᶜat Dār al-Kutub wa-Būlāq.

Amālī = *Al-Amālī*, Dār al-Kutub.

Arabic Morphology = *Arabic Morphology and Phonology based on the Marāḥ al-arwāḥ by Ahmad b. Ali b. Masud*, Joyce Åkesson, Brill 2001.

Basṭ = *Basṭ sāmiᶜ al-masāmir*, nr 375 of the Taymūrīya collections *(majāmīᶜ taymūrīya)* in Dār al-Kutub.

Dikt = Svensk dikt från trollformler till Lars Norén, en antologi sammanställd av docent Lars Gustafsson, Stockholm 1978 - Great Brittain 1980.

Dīwān = *Dīwān majnūn Leylā,* ed. ᶜAbd al-Sattār Aḥmad Farrāj, Dār miṣr lil-ṭibāᶜā.

Khizāna = *Khizānat al-adab li-l-Baghdādī*, Būlāq 1299.

Les Fleurs du Mal = Les Fleurs du Mal et autres poèmes, Ch. Baudelaire, Paris 1964.

Masālik = Masālik al-abṣār, a Manuscript in Dār al-Kutub.

Maṣāri^c = Maṣāri^c al-^cushshāq, Maṭba^cat al-Jawā'ib 1301 A.H.

Samṭ = Samṭ al-la'ālī, Maṭba^cat lajnat al-ta'līf.

Ṣifat jazīrat al-^carab = Ṣifat jazīrat al-^carab, Ḥamdāni, Ed. D. H. Müller, Leiden 1968.

Tārīkh Baghdād, Maṭba^cat as-Sa^cāda 1349 A.H.

Tazyīn = Tazyīn al-aswāq, al-Maṭba^ca al-Azharīya 1328, 3rd edition.

The Flowers of Evil, William Aggeler, Guild, 1954.

Zahra = Az-Zahra, Beirut 1351.

Index of Arabic Verses

164

أيا قبر ليلى لو شهدناك أعولت (60)

أيا ليلى بكى لي بعينيك رحمة (21)

بحبك يا ليلى قد أصبحت شهرة (3)

بنفسي من لا بد لي أن أهاجره (34)

تذكرت ليلى والسنين الخواليا (58)

حججت ولم أحجج لذنب جنيته (43)

حلال لليلى شتمنا وانتقاصنا (49)

ذكرتك حيث استأمن الوحش (45)

ذكرتك والحجيج لهم ضجيج (44)

رعاة الليل ما فعل الصباح (27)

زها جسم ليلى في الثياب تنعما (10)

سلبت عظامي لحمها فتركتها (53)

عجبت لليلى كيف نامت وقد غفت (56)

فوالله ثم والله إني لدائب (30)

فيا قلب مت حزنا ولا تك جازعا (29)

لو سيل أهل الهوى من بعد موتهم (61)

ليالي أصبو بالعشي وبالضحى (11)

(51) ما بال قلبك يا مجنون قد خلعا

(47) متى يشتفي منك الفؤاد المعذب

(24) مليحة أطلال العشيات لو بدت

(6) منعت عن التسليم يوم وداعها

(54) نظرت كأني من وراء زجاجة

(12) هي الخمر فى حسن وكالخمر ريقها

(15) وأجهشت للتوباد حين رأيته

(50) وأنت التي كلفتني دلج السرى

(37) وإنك لو بلغتها قولي اسلمى

(33) وجدت الحب نيرانا تلظى

(42) وداع دعا إذ نحن بالخيف من منى

(1) وقالوا لو تشاء سلوت عنها

(55) وقفت لليلى بعد عشرين حجة

(9) وما الناس إلا العاشقون ذو الهوى

(13) ومما شجاني أنها يوم ودعت

(25) يقولون ليلى بالعراق مريضة

(20) يقولون لي يوما وقد جئت حيهم

(35) يميل بي الهوى في أرض ليلى

Printed in Great Britain
by Amazon

33227990R00106